Women's and Children's Legal Rights Handbook

W. Stratton Treadway

Triangle Books

Triangle Books
are published by
Research Triangle Publishing, Inc.
PO Box 1223
Fuquay-Varina, NC 27526

ISBN 1-884570-18-6

Library of Congress Catalog Card Number: 94-80058

Printed in the United States of America
10 9 8 7 6 5 4 3 2 1

I dedicate this handbook to my mother,

Rita B. Treadway

"Mom, I'm always thinking of you"

REST IN PEACE

Acknowledgments

Regina—Without whom this book would never have been written.

Matt—For lending me the computer and because he asked me to.

Bill & Kevin—For the encouragement and understanding that children seldom have.

Wendy—For her time and word processing skills.

Contents

INTRODUCTION

This book is intended as a general summary of women's and children's legal rights in the United States in the hope that the knowledge contained in these pages will contribute to a better and safer life for all women and children.

In recent years, through the hard work of countless individuals and organizations concerned with women's and children's rights, courts and legislatures have taken many steps to strengthen the guarantees of equal opportunity and equality of everyday life for women, children and minorities in our society. These guarantees can, will and are being improved upon by continuing to understand the problems unique to women, children and minorities, and by making these rights understood by all. My hope is to assist in the endeavor of still further improving the lives and security of all concerned.

While women will find this book of special interest, much of the information concerns laws prohibiting discrimination on the basis of race, color, religion, age and physical handicap, as well as sex and sexual preference. Therefore, this book will be useful to all American citizens who wish to protect themselves and care about the fair and equal treatment of people in employment, economic transactions, housing, business establishments and other areas.

In this book, I have tried to provide as much detailed information as possible about your rights, and to cover the laws of all fifty states, as well as the laws of the federal government. State and federal laws are different in content and intent. I have selected laws and statutes common to the majority of the states. I have also selected certain federal laws which in many cases establish the basis for individual state laws and statutes. The laws of your state of residence may be different, but by using this book as a guide, you will easily be able to determine your rights based on state law through a simple telephone call to the agency or organization affected.

We live in an increasingly litigious society. Our laws are complicated. This book does not replace the need for legal counsel in certain situations. While it can help you understand your rights, any author would be remiss not to recommend that you seek legal counsel before you take steps that could have serious legal consequences.

CHAPTER 1

EMPLOYMENT

Employment discrimination is generally illegal except where specifically indicated by law. There are both federal and state laws prohibiting the imposition of discriminatory conditions of employment by employers, employment agencies, labor organizations and training programs. However, federal and state laws that prohibit employment discrimination differ in scope and with respect to the groups covered and actions outlawed.

Title V11 of the Civil Rights Act is the federal law that is applicable to most cases of employment discrimination. Title V11 applies to employers with fifteen or more employees and outlaws discrimination based on race, color, religion, sex or national origin. Some states have their own laws that are broader in scope than Title V11. These differences can include the addition of discrimination based on age (over a certain age), national origin, ancestry, physical handicap, medical condition (controlled cancer), marital status or sexual preference. Employers with fewer than fifteen employees may be effected in your state by local law. According to the Rehabilitation Act of 1973, employers who receive federal funds are also prohibited from discrimination on the basis of handicap.

The Equal Pay Act of 1963 is also an integral part of the protection of women's employment rights. The Equal Pay Act does exactly as the title suggests. It guarantees equal pay for equal work. This law demands that women and men be treated fairly and equally when applying for a job, and in all aspects of the job—hiring, firing, wages and benefits, training and advancement through promotion or transfer. The law says there cannot be different pay scales for male and female employees who perform equal work. That is, jobs performed under similar working conditions that require the same skills, effort and responsibilities must be equally compensated. The law outlaws employment practices that treat male and female employees unequally, and practices that appear neutral but have a negative impact on the employment of men and women.

Federal and state laws that prohibit discrimination in employment deal with a whole range of employment issues from hiring practices to retirement age. This chapter discusses the organizations covered by these laws. It explains illegal discriminatory hiring practices, and describes a few instances in which discriminatory hiring is legal. It also discusses legal guarantees of equality of employment benefits and working conditions. Finally, this section describes resources to contract if you feel that you have been discriminated against and have decided to seek a legal solution.

ORGANIZATIONS COVERED

Laws prohibiting discriminatory actions with respect to employment are not limited to discrimination by employers. They also cover discrimination by labor unions, employment agencies and training programs. The purpose of this section is to point out potential employment practices which are discriminatory and therefore illegal.

EMPLOYERS: It is generally unlawful for an employer to engage in any of the following practices on the basis of your sex:
- Refusing to hire you.
- Refusing to select you for an apprenticeship program.
- Refusing to choose you to go through a training program which leads to being hired.
- Firing you.
- Paying you less.
- Denying you benefits.
- Discriminating against you in any way.

LABOR ORGANIZATIONS: It is generally unlawful for a labor organization to engage in any of the following practices because of your sex:
- Refusing you or excluding you from membership.
- Providing you with an inferior membership.

- Refusing to allow you to participate in elections of officers, staff or organizers.
- Refusing to allow you to participate in the union at the officeholder level.
- Discriminating against you in any way.

EMPLOYMENT AGENCIES: It is generally unlawful for an employment agency to engage in any of the following practices on the basis of your sex:

- Refusing to allow you to apply for a particular position.
- Refusing to refer you to a potential employer.
- Discriminating against you in any way.

TRAINING PROGRAMS: All of the discriminatory practices usually illegal for an employer are also illegal for training programs. Therefore, it is generally illegal for a training program to engage in any of the following practices on the basis of sex:

- Refusing to hire you.
- Refusing to select you for an apprenticeship program.
- Refusing to allow you to go through a training program which leads to being hired.
- Taking you out of a training program which leads to being hired.
- Firing you.
- Paying you less.
- Denying you benefits.
- Discriminating against you in any way.

Some states require apprenticeship training programs to include women within their affirmative action plans. For more information on apprenticeship training programs, contact your State Unemployment Office.

UNLAWFUL DISCRIMINATION IN HIRING

From the moment you start looking for work, you are covered by the laws that make employment discrimination illegal. Job and help wanted advertisements are for men and women. It is illegal for an employer, advertising agency or union to advertise for only male or only female job applicants unless being male or female is absolutely necessary to job performance. If you are looking for a job, you are legally entitled to apply for any job for which you believe you are qualified.

Employment agencies must refer all qualified applicants. It is unlawful for an employment or placement agency to discriminate in job referrals against a woman solely on the basis of her sex. A woman must be referred to all job listings whose requirements meet her qualifications.

Company hiring departments must interview equally. When an employer has its own "company" or internal hiring department, it may be unlawful for an employer to fill job openings by relying solely on the recommendations of its own employees. This is especially true in those businesses with work forces made up mostly of white men. This would constitute a practice that might appear to be neutral but which is prohibited because it freezes the status quo for prior discriminatory employment practices and has a disparate impact on minorities.

If an employer considers prior work experience when hiring or promoting, unpaid volunteer work experience must also be considered.

JOB APPLICATIONS: When you apply for a job, most employers will ask you to fill out a questionnaire or job application form. The form may ask questions such as whether you are male or female, or married or single, and the form can ask you to list your height and weight. Such questions are lawful as long as they are asked of all job applicants, and as long as the information is used for legitimate job-screening or record-keeping purposes and not used to discriminate against you. An employer may only ask questions about your health that are directly related to the working conditions of the job involved. Once you are hired, an employer may ask for additional information needed for insurance or other fringe benefit programs. That information may not be used in a discriminatory manner.

An employer may not ask you questions about childbearing, pregnancy, birth control or family responsibilities unless they are related to specific and relevant working conditions of the job in question.

JOB REQUIREMENTS: With only a few exceptions, it is unlawful for an employer to set requirements for employment that would restrict those eligible to only male or only female applicants (the few legal exceptions are listed and explained in the section, Lawful Discrimination in Employment). An employer may not refuse to consider your application for employment simply because he or she assumes that women are not physically able to do the job in question.

The use of minimum height and weight restrictions are limited to cases where such restrictions are clearly necessary for safe and efficient job performance. An employer may not use differential height and weight requirements for men and women unless pursuant to a permissible defense, such as a bona fide occupational qualification.

An employer may not make generalizations about physical ability or sex. An employer may not refuse to hire a woman for a particular job solely because the employer believes that women are "too weak" for the job. You have a right to demonstrate your capability to perform a job.

An employer may not discriminate against a particular gender because of customer preference. It is unlawful for an employer to have a policy of hiring only men because its customers do not like being served by women.

An employer may not discriminate against a particular gender because of traditional job classifications. A hospital may not refuse to hire male nurses just because nursing is traditionally a female occupation.

An employer may not discriminate against one gender because the work place has facilities for only one gender. An employer may not refuse to hire women because there are no women's bathrooms on the premises.

An employer may not refuse to hire an applicant because she is of childbearing age.

Although an employer may ask on a job application if you are married or single, the employer may not consider your marital status when deciding whether to hire you. Marital status information may be required for gathering additional information about you, for such reasons as credit reports, contacting friends or relatives, or to verify your identity and any disclosures you may have made. An employment application may ask whether you have ever used another name, but this information must be used only for checking your past work experience or for other non-discriminatory purposes.

An application may ask whether your spouse is currently employed by that same employer. However, this information may not be used in determining whether you should be hired unless the particular job presents problems of security, supervision, morale or safety if both spouses are employed by the same employer. An employer may refuse to place both spouses in the same department if the employer can show that such placement would cause supervision, safety, security or morale problems that would be greater than problems caused by the placement of persons other than married couples.

An employer may not generally refuse to hire or employ a job applicant based on his or her religious beliefs. Discrimination against an employee or job applicant due to conflict between any employment requirement and an employee's religious beliefs is generally unlawful. However, if the employer has explored alternative means of accommodating the religious belief or observance and is unable to accommodate the employee without undue hardship on the business, the employer is not required to accommodate the employee. Personal or vacation time would have to be used for religious observances if undo hardships on the company were a problem.

An employer may not refuse to hire a job applicant because the applicant has a physical handicap, so long as the applicant can perform the job safely.

An employer may not generally refuse to hire a job applicant because the applicant is over the age of forty.

Citizenship requirements that have the purpose or effect of discriminating against applicants or employees on the basis of national origin or ancestry are unlawful unless pursuant to one of the defenses permitted by Title V11 of the Civil Rights Act. Aliens who feel that they have been discriminated against may file charges of discrimination pursuant to Title V11, after they have filed form 1-772 with the Immigration and Naturalization Service, declaring their intention to become citizens. It is not necessary for them to have filed the form before the discrimination has occurred. However, if they do not intend to become citizens, Title V11 does not protect them against discrimination by an employer.

LAWFUL DISCRIMINATION IN EMPLOYMENT

There are rare circumstances in which an employer may discriminate. These practices are lawful only if there are no less discriminatory alternative practices available. Examples of discrimination that may be lawful follow.

BONA FIDE OCCUPATIONAL QUALIFICATIONS: An employer may discriminate against an entire group of people if it can be shown that the practice is justified because certain people are not able to safely and efficiently perform the job. The employer must prove that the discrimination is necessary to serve the legitimate nature of the business. Privacy considerations are an example of a bona fide occupational qualification. If the job requires an employee to observe others in a state of nudity or conduct body searches, then the employer may possibly limit the job to members of the sex to be observed or searched. However, job duties involving such activities must be assigned so as to maximize the number of jobs for which either men or women are eligible. For example, in a prison environment, allowing male officers to view female inmates in partial or total nudity does not violate inmates' rights of privacy if male contact is minimal, professional and necessary to further the correctional system's legitimate goals and policies.

AFFIRMATIVE ACTION PLANS: Bona fide affirmative action may be a valid defense to employment actions that would otherwise be unlawful discrimination. An employer may adopt a voluntary affirmative action plan for example, setting aside a certain number of new trainee positions for women or minorities, so long as the affirmative action program meets certain tests set by the U.S. Supreme Court: "A bona fide affirmative action plan must break down traditional discriminatory practices without unnecessarily interfering with the rights of other employees. Such a plan must be narrowly tailored to the achievement of its goal of remedying past discrimination, must not operate as an absolute bar to others and should be of limited duration."

VETERANS: Veterans' preference laws have been held legal and veterans' preference is expressly permitted under law.

EQUALITY OF WORKING CONDITIONS

Federal and state laws prohibit sex discrimination with regard to either the conditions of your work place or the employment benefits you receive. If rest periods are provided, the conditions and amount of time must be equal for both sexes. Equal access to comparable toilet facilities must be provided to employees of both sexes. However, locks may be installed on common facilities to insure privacy. An employer may not assign job duties according to a person's sex or sexual preference. And, an employer may not consider a person's sex when providing clerical assistance, office space or any other support service.

EQUAL PAY

Federal and state laws guarantee equal pay for equal work. You cannot be paid less than a man because of your sex. It is unlawful for an employer to pay you less because you are not the principal wage earner or head of your household. Likewise, it is unlawful for an employer to condition the availability of fringe benefits on whether you are the head of your household.

Health plans, however, may provide greater benefits to employees with dependents than to those without dependents or to those with fewer dependents.

SEXUAL HARASSMENT IN THE WORK PLACE

You have an absolute right to be free from sexual harassment related to your employment. Such harassment does not have to be outright or obvious to be illegal. (Conduct which implies that sexual demands are being made such as verbal, symbolic or pictorial gestures that make work difficult for you are illegal. Moreover, the law demands that employers take all reasonable steps to prevent sexual harassment in the work place.)

(The Civil Rights Act of 1964, which sets guidelines on discrimination because of sex, defines this behavior as "unwelcome sexual advances, requests for sexual favors, and other verbal or physical conduct of a sexual nature when submission to such conduct is either explicitly or implicitly a term or condition of an individual's employment." Sexual harassment occurs either when submission to or rejection of the sexual advances are the basis for employment decisions affecting a person or when the sexual overtures have the purpose or effect of unreasonably interfering with an individual's work performance by creating an intimidating, hostile or offensive working environment.)

Sex discrimination in any educational program or activity receiving federal financial assistance is illegal. (The Civil Rights Act of 1964 prohibits discrimination on the basis of race or national origin in programs receiving federal financial assistance.) (The U.S. Department of Justice and the U.S. Department of Education are charged with the major responsibilities of enforcing the laws set forth in this act.) With certain exceptions, this act bars sex discrimination in any academic, athletic, extracurricular, vocational, research, occupational training or other educational program—public or private, preschool to postgraduate—operated by a school district, governing body, organization or agency which receives or benefits from federal aid.

Exempted from the provisions of this law are:

- Schools whose primary purpose is the training of the U.S. Military services or the Merchant Marine.
- Admissions policies of public undergraduate institutions which have traditionally had a policy of excluding members of one sex.
- Practices in schools controlled by religious organizations whenever compliance would contravene their religious beliefs.
- Membership policies of the Girl Scouts and Boy Scouts, the YMCA and the YWCA, Campfire Girls and other single-sex, tax-exempt youth service organizations whose members are primarily under age nineteen.
- Activities relating to the American Legions' Boys State, Boys Nation, Girls State and Girls Nation conferences.
- Father-son, mother-daughter activities as long as opportunities for reasonably comparable activities are offered to students of both sexes.
- Scholarships or other aid offered by colleges and universities to participants in single-sex pageants which reward the combination of personal appearance, poise and talent.

Regulations of the act do not require that school athletic programs for girls be an exact duplicate of those already in place for boys; they were intended to encourage the development of an alternative program depending on the needs and interests of female students.

The Women's Educational Equity Act of 1984 provides federal grants (up to $40,000) to provide educational equity for women and girls who suffer multiple discrimination, bias or stereotyping based on sex and race, ethnic origin, disability or age.

PREGNANCY

The law guarantees that women affected by childbirth or related medical conditions must be treated the same for all employment-related purposes, including the receipt of fringe benefits, as other persons with similar ability or inability to work.

The Pregnancy Discrimination Act prohibits discrimination against pregnant women in any area of employment, including hiring, promotion, seniority rights and job security. This amendment requires public and private sector employers who offer health insurance and temporary disability plans to provide coverage to women for pregnancy, childbirth and related medical conditions. The amendment is generally neutral on the subject of abortion coverage. Coverage for abortion is not required, except where the life of the mother would be endangered if the fetus were carried to term or where medical conditions have resulted from abortion.

You cannot be discriminated against because of a pregnancy-related condition. A working pregnant woman has the right to the same benefits and privileges of employment as a working person who is not pregnant as long as they are similar in their ability to work. It is unlawful for an employer to fire you, refuse you a promotion, reduce your pay or reduce your benefits and privileges of employment solely because of pregnancy, childbirth or a medical condition related to pregnancy or childbirth.

An employer may not limit disability benefits for pregnancy-related conditions to married employees. In addition, an employer absolutely may not require you to be sterilized as a condition of employment.

PREGNANCY AND LEAVES OF ABSENCE: The Family Leave and Medical Leave Act grants unpaid leaves of up to twelve weeks to workers for the birth or adoption of a child or the illness of a close family member. If you need to take time off for childbirth, to adopt a child, to care for a child, spouse or parent with a serious health condition, or for your own serious illness, you may do so once for twelve weeks during any twelve-month period.

You must have worked for the same employer for at least one year and for at least 1,230 hours during the period you need to take your leave, and you must not be one of the top ten percent of the highest paid employees at the company for which you work.

Your employer may grant you the twelve weeks leave per the requirements for the Family and Medical Leave Act if you are among the top ten percent of the highest paid employees and if you are not considered a key employee whose leave would result in "substantial and grievous economic injury" to the business.

If you take an unpaid leave under the guidelines of the Family and Medical Leave Act, your employer must continue your health insurance coverage and guarantee your old job or a comparable position paying the same wage as your previous job.

PREGNANCY AND EMPLOYER PROVIDED INSUR-ANCE: An employer must give equal treatment to all employees to the extent that health insurance protection is provided by the employer. If a health insurance plan covers the cost of a private room for pregnancy-related conditions, it must provide the same for other conditions. If the plan covers office visits to doctors for other conditions, it must cover prenatal and postnatal visits for pregnant women.

If an employer's medical insurance plan covers the medical expenses of husbands of female employees, it must also cover the medical expenses, including pregnancy, of wives of male employees.

Employers who have less than fifty employees and offer health insurance and temporary disability plans to provide coverage to women for pregnancy, childbirth and related medical conditions must grant unpaid leave to employees for other medical conditions.

If your employer allows sick-leave pay during any length of illness for an employee, you may use part of or all of your sick pay due you when you take your medical leave.

PREGNANCY AND HAZARDOUS WORK CONDI-TIONS: It may be unlawful for an employer to deny the request of a pregnant employee to be transferred to a less strenuous or hazardous position when the employer has a practice of transferring temporarily disabled employees to less hazardous positions for the duration of their disability. Even in the absence of such a policy, it may be unlawful for an employer to refuse to transfer a pregnant employee to a less hazardous position for the duration of the pregnancy, provided the request for transfer can be reasonably accommodated by the employer. If the transfer forces the employer to create additional employment that would not otherwise have been created, discharge an employee with more seniority or promote an employee who is not qualified to perform a job, then the employer will not be required to facilitate such a transfer.

If you have been transferred to a less strenuous or hazardous position for the duration of your pregnancy, you must not be penalized for the transfer when you return to your original job. This means that you must be allowed to return to your original job or a similar one, with no loss of seniority or decrease in pay.

An employer who wants to protect an employee's unborn children from hazardous employment may not exclude all women of childbearing age. However, the employer may determine if its hazards affect the reproductive systems of either men or women or both men and women. If the conditions are hazardous to either men or women or both men and women of childbearing age, the employer must transfer the employee, unless to do so would impose an undue hardship, or must eliminate or minimize the number of hazardous working conditions.

A fetal protection policy will not be upheld unless an employer shows:

- The existence of a substantial risk of harm to employees' offspring through the exposure of employees to a reproductive or fetal hazard in the work place.
- That the harm to employees' offspring takes place through the exposure of employees of only one sex.
- That the employer's policy effectively eliminates the risk of fetal or reproductive harm.

Even if the above elements are proved, an employer's policy will be unacceptable if a reasonable alternative policy exists that will protect employees' offspring from fetal or reproductive harm and that will have a less discriminatory impact on employees of the restricted sex.

An employee may refuse, for safety reasons, to perform a task that is assigned. No employee may be laid off or discharged for refusing to perform work in which the labor code, any occupational or health standard or any safety order will be violated where the violation would create a real and apparent hazard to the employee or his or her fellow employees.

Employees have a right to request an immediate inspection by the Occupational Safety and Health Act Division (OSHA) of the U.S. Department of Labor or their local State Occupational Safety Department, if they believe that hazardous conditions exist in their work place or if they believe they are in imminent danger.

Workers who are injured on the job or who contract a disease directly connected with their occupation can seek relief under state workers' compensation laws. In most states, employers are required to cover employees with this protection and heavy penalties are assessed for failure to comply. Your State Department of Labor can help you solve any problems with filing a claim. You may also want to talk to a lawyer.

Several cities and states have enacted laws requiring employers to inform employees about toxic substances to which they are exposed at a work site. Also, your union can request a list of all chemicals and other substances to which the workers they represent are exposed.

ABORTION (EMPLOYMENT RELATED)

You may not be discriminated against because you have had an abortion. All fringe benefits other than health insurance that are provided for other medical conditions must also be provided for abortion. For example, if your employer provided sick leave in case of other medical conditions, sick leave must also be provided in case of abortion.

State medical leave laws may grant medical leave for an abortion. In some states, employers are required to provide coverage in their health insurance plans for abortions in which carrying the fetus to term would endanger the mother or where medical complications have arisen from an abortion.

If you are in the military and you request an abortion at a military medical facility, anywhere in the world, you are entitled to receive that abortion at no charge to you.

If you require counseling in a federally funded family planning clinic, you may not be denied that counseling.

SEXUAL ORIENTATION

It is illegal, in most cases and in all states, for employers to discriminate against a person in employment opportunities on the basis of a person's sexual orientation. The exceptions deal with military policy. Discriminating against any employee because of his or her political affiliation has been construed by some states to prohibit employment discrimination on the basis of sexual orientation.

Some cities and counties also have local ordinances prohibiting discrimination on the basis of sexual orientation. Check with your city attorney, county counsel or another lawyer.

It is illegal for government employers and privately owned utility companies to discriminate in employment on the basis of a person's sexual orientation. The equal protection clause of the United States Constitution has been held to prohibit state and privately owned utility companies from discrimination in employment opportunities based on sexual orientation.

UNEMPLOYMENT INSURANCE

Courts in approximately forty states now recognize some exemptions to the common-law doctrine that non-union employees can be fired arbitrarily. In these states, employees who believe they have been fired unlawfully may be able to sue for wrongful discharge. Some states have laws that prohibit being discharged for refusing to engage in illegal activity or refusing to testify in court. Some states also protect employees from being fired for serving on a jury, refusing to take lie detector tests or for filing any claims of discrimination.

When an employee leaves a job voluntarily, they are not entitled to receive unemployment insurance in most states. To be eligible, a person must be unemployed, able to work and available for and seeking work. Unemployment compensation laws prohibit states from refusing benefits to women solely on the basis of pregnancy.

Quitting without good cause and being fired for misconduct are the two reasons for denying unemployment compensation. Women who have left jobs because of sexual harassment have won challenges and received unemployment insurance. Also, some states will pay benefits to persons who have to quit their jobs for compelling personal reasons. Examples of compelling reasons are health problems due to chemical or chronic reactions to a work environment and relocation with a spouse who is the major wage earner. Decisions in these cases are made according to individual circumstances.

Some states will consider persons who can only work part time as available and eligible for unemployment insurance if they have been working part time in an occupation where there is a substantial demand for workers.

The U.S. Employment Service operates in partnership with state employment agencies to provide free counseling, testing and job placement in major cities across the country. Through screening and referral services, the job service, which should be listed in the telephone directory under "State Government" listings, channels applicants into various training programs.

The National Labor Relation Act of 1935 (amended) guarantees employees the right to organize, to bargain collectively and to engage in strikes, picketing and other organized activities for their mutual aid and protection. It also guarantees the right of any employee to refrain from these activities. The act makes it an unfair labor practice for employers to interfere with employees in the exercise of these rights, to discriminate against them in hiring, firing or any term or condition of employment because they have engaged in activities protected by the act.

EMPLOYMENT RIGHTS OF OLDER WOMEN

The Fair Employment and Housing Act prohibits discrimination on the basis of sex and age. However, many older women do feel doubly disadvantaged in the job market. There are organizations that help women over forty who feel that they have been discriminated against or who are trying to gain reentry into the job market. See the Directory of Services and Information at the end of this book for a listing of state offices responsible for developing programs and policies benefiting older women and national legal programs specializing in the legal problems of the elderly.

RETIREMENT

An employer may not discriminate with respect to retirement benefits on the basis of sex. In addition, an employer may not have different optional retirement ages for men and women.

FIRING

An employer may not fire you on the basis of your sex, race, religion, color, age or for any other discriminatory reason. You should check your state laws regarding firing as they vary from state to state.

LEGAL REMEDIES

If you believe that an employer has discriminated against you in any condition of employment because of your sex, race, marital status, religion, color, national origin, ancestry, physical handicap, medical condition (controlled cancer), or denied you equal pay, contact one of the government agencies listed in the directory at the end of this book. You can also locate your local government agencies through your local telephone book or contact a lawyer for advice and legal assistance. An agency representative or lawyer may be able to help you become reinstated or obtain money to compensate you for lost wages, emotional distress or other issues.

An employer, labor organization or employment agency may not retaliate against you because you have opposed its discriminatory practices or because you have assisted in bringing or actually brought legal action against it. If retaliatory action has been brought against you, the law gives you the right to sue to recover damages. If you decide to seek legal counsel, it is important that you act promptly. There are stringent legal time limitations on filing complaints about employment discrimination.

CHAPTER 2

ECONOMIC INDEPENDENCE

State and federal laws generally provide for equal treatment of men and women in the economic sphere. Chapter One dealt exclusively with employment issues. This chapter discusses women's rights with respect to a wider range of economic issues. Specific topics in this chapter include credit, bill collectors, business establishments, contracts, insurance and public assistance programs.

CREDIT

Any business, such as a bank or gasoline company, that extends credit for goods or services is a "creditor." A combination of state and federal laws makes it unlawful for a creditor to refuse to extend credit or allow the exercise of certain legal rights to a person because of his or her sex, marital status, race, color, national origin, religion, age or receipt of public assistance (with limited exceptions).

According to the law, a woman, whether married or single, is entitled to have credit accounts kept in her own name so that she has a separate credit history and can establish a good credit rating in her own name. When credit is denied to any person, that person has a right to a written statement of the reasons for the denial from the creditor. That person also has a right to a copy of his or her own credit history report from the "credit reporting bureau" that the creditor used when refusing to extend credit.

A person or group of people may file a legal action against a creditor who discriminated illegally. If discrimination by a creditor is proved in court, the court may award actual damages, punitive damages and attorneys' fees against the creditor.

DISCRIMINATION: Discrimination in granting credit is generally illegal. However, creditors are allowed to determine your credit worthiness on the basis of your income, expenses, debts and reliability.

If you are an unmarried woman, you must be treated as an unmarried man would be treated when you apply for credit. If you have earnings and assets that meet the creditor's requirements, you must be given the same credit by that store or bank as a man in your position would be given. Federal guidelines allow a creditor to inquire about marital status if you live in a community property state like California (see Chapter Seven). In community property states, unless otherwise agreed upon, all property that is acquired by you or your spouse through either of your labor or skills during the term of marriage is deemed to be "community property" and each spouse therefore owns one-half of all community property.

If you are a married woman, you must be treated as a man (married or single) would be treated when you apply for credit. You may have more earnings and other assets under your management and control than a single working woman because of your husband's job and your community property. However, a credit agency must grant you credit, in your own name, just as it would give a man in your position.

BILLING ERRORS: Retailers and card issuers must correct billing errors made by them within sixty days. If they willfully refuse to do so, the cardholder may be able to collect three times his or her actual damages, along with reasonable attorneys' fees and costs.

CREDIT HISTORY: To get credit, you must show the creditor that you are "credit worthy." Being credit worthy means that you have a separate credit history identifying you as a person who has managed your earnings and assets and has borrowed and repaid your debts on time. One way to start a credit history is to open a checking or savings account in your own name. You may then apply to your bank for a bank credit card in your own name. If you charge purchases on your bank card and repay your bills on time, you will have a basis to prove your credit worthiness. As your credit history continues, you may be able to increase your credit limits and open additional credit accounts. You might also wish to open a charge account in your own name in a retail store. Obviously, you should use credit only if you can afford to repay your debts.

You may create a credit history for yourself by establishing accounts in your name. Your own legal name is your personal first name and the last name (maiden name or married name) that you prefer to use. For example, if you were born "Mary Smith" and you married "Bill Jones," you may use as your own name "Mary Smith" or "Mary Jones" or "Mary Smith Jones." Any of these names will create your own credit identity. However, if you are married and you keep your bank account and credit cards in the name of "Mrs. Bill Jones," you have not created your own credit identity. You have duplicated your husband's identity, since "Mrs. Bill Jones" is merely a social title.

Joint accounts usually help establish your own credit history. All joint accounts opened after January 1977 are required by law to be reported in both the husband's and wife's names. For any joint charge account of a married couple opened before 1977 you have the right to request that the creditor (store, business, etc.) report the joint account in both names, i.e., "Bill and Mary Jones." You should request that the creditor report the credit history on the joint account in both names to the credit reporting bureau.

CREDIT REPORTING BUREAUS: You can verify your separate credit history by getting a copy of your credit history report from a credit reporting bureau. Sometimes called a "credit bureau" or "credit reporting agency," they are clearinghouses that provide subscriber members (banks, stores, businesses) with information about the financial transactions of their customers. The information available from a credit reporting bureau comes from the same subscriber members who report to the bureau delinquent debts, civil judgments, bankruptcies and collections against their own customers. A bureau records and maintains this information, usually on computer. A bureau usually does not do any independent investigation of the information reported to it by subscriber members.

To find out if you have a credit history and to see a copy of your own credit history reports, ask your bank or other creditor the name and address of the credit reporting bureau that they use.

You have the right to get a copy (for a small fee) of your own credit history report from a credit reporting bureau at any time. If you have been denied credit, you may usually get a copy of your credit history report without charge by requesting it within thirty days after you are denied credit. You also can obtain the names of any other recipients of your credit reports within a certain time period, usually one year.

If the information in your own credit history report is out of date, incorrect or in dispute, you should put in writing all necessary corrections and return the corrected report to the bureau. The bureau is required to check the new information, and if correct, change your credit history report. You may request that the corrected information be sent to any creditor who received a negative report in the past six months, and to prospective employers who received a negative report during the prior two years.

If a credit reporting bureau decides that it disagrees with you, it must notify you within five days of its decision that it believes your dispute is groundless and state reasons why it will not reinvestigate your report. If this happens, you may file your own statement of 100 words or less presenting your side of the story, and this statement must be included in your credit history report.

CREDIT APPLICATIONS: When you apply for credit, you will probably be asked to fill out a written credit application. It is illegal for a creditor to make any discriminatory statements discouraging you from applying for credit.

It is illegal for a creditor to issue you a credit card unless you have specifically requested one, or unless it is a renewal of or a substitution for an accepted credit card.

There are a number of questions that credit applications usually ask. When filling out an application for credit, you will probably be asked about your employment, monthly earnings, savings and checking accounts, other credit accounts, dependents, whether you own or rent your house or apartment and how long you have resided there and your telephone numbers at home and work. Such questions are lawful. Generally, creditors are looking for information to establish whether you appear to have the stability in terms of job, home and residence in the community to indicate that you are a good credit risk.

Creditors may ask you limited questions about your marital status. They may ask whether you are married, unmarried or separated. They may not ask whether you are divorced or widowed. This information may be used only to evaluate your credit worthiness, not to discriminate against you. The application may ask you to designate a title such as "Ms." or "Mrs.," but you are not required to give this information. A creditor is legally permitted to ask you about your immigration status when you apply for credit.

There are a limited number of questions a creditor may ask you about your children. A creditor may ask you how many children you have now who are your dependents. However, this information may be used only to determine your financial situation, and not for discriminatory reasons. For example, a creditor cannot discriminate against you because you are a single parent.

There are a number of questions that are illegal for you to be asked when filling out a credit application. These include questions about your birth control practices, how many children you plan to have or adopt, whether you are able to have children, your race, color, religion, national origin, sex or age. If you are married, you may apply for credit in your own name. All credit applications must tell you that you have a right to a separate account regardless of the fact that you are married. Usually, your signature alone will be required on the credit application if you apply for separate credit.

If you are married, you may use your maiden name when applying for credit. You have a right to use either your husband's name or your maiden (birth) name on your credit card. You may not be discriminated against because you choose to use your maiden name.

If you are married, you may be asked questions about your spouse when applying for joint credit. Because some states are community property states (see Chapter Seven), you may be asked to give information about your spouse when applying for joint credit, or when alimony or support payments from your spouse or former spouse will be relied upon as a source of information for repayment of your debts.

If asked, you must usually disclose debts against your community property when you apply for credit. A creditor may ask you to provide information about any debts that you and your husband have against your community property. This means that you may be asked about debts incurred by your husband even if you are seeking credit only in your name. This is because each spouse is responsible for the community debts of the marriage.

A creditor may not use this information to discriminate against you just because you are a woman. This means that an application for credit cannot ask you questions that it does not ask a man in your situation.

You cannot be forced to reapply for credit if you get a divorce. If you change your marital status or your name, you may not be forced to reapply for a credit card you already have. The only time a creditor may either cancel your credit card or reduce your limit after a change in your marital status is when you are either unable or unwilling to pay your debts. This means that your credit cards may not be canceled simply because you are divorced, widowed or because you change your name.

You do not have to give any information about alimony, child support or separate maintenance payments unless you want the amounts from those sources to be included as part of your income. This means that if you do not want the creditor to know that you are divorced and are receiving alimony payments, you should not include these payments as part of your income on the credit application. On the other hand, if you have no other sources of income, you will want your alimony payments to be included in your income, and you may have to disclose the source of those payments.

It is unlawful for a creditor to discriminate against you because you are living with a man to whom you are not married.

CREDIT DENIAL: If you are denied credit, you have the right to be informed of the exact reasons for denial. Once you have filed a written application for credit, you have a right to a written explanation from the creditor if you are turned down.

After you have applied for credit, you must be informed whether you have been given or denied credit within thirty days after the creditor received your completed application. The creditor must either:

- Give you a statement of specific reasons for denying credit to you, or
- Give you the name, address and telephone number of the person who can tell you the reasons you were denied credit. The reasons must be sent to you within sixty days after receiving your request.

A creditor who fails to supply a credit applicant with the reason for the denial for credit is liable for any actual damages sustained by the applicant as a result of the failure.

If you have been denied credit by any creditor, the notice of denial must give you the name and address of the credit reporting bureau that supplied your credit history. You may want to review your credit report by contacting the credit report bureau in your city. You can find out about your credit history report by pursuing one of these options:

- Going to the credit reporting bureau in person, presenting identification and requesting a copy of your file. The agency must then give you a copy of your file. If the agency uses codes, you must be given an explanation of the codes used.
- Writing a letter to the bureau requesting a decoded version of your file. You must present proper identification in your letter and give a specific mailing address.
- Writing a letter requesting that the credit reporting bureau call you and give you the information in your file. Your letter must give identification and your telephone number.
- The credit reporting bureau may charge you the cost of the telephone call.

If you were denied credit and you request a copy of the information in your file within thirty days of denial, you will not usually be charged a service fee. However, if your file requires preparation of special material, you may be charged a reasonable service fee.

If you request a copy of your file not pursuant to a credit denial, you may be charged a reasonable service charge. You may not be charged more than a certain amount (usually $8.00) to get a copy of your credit history file.

The following information generally must not be included in a consumer credit report:

- Bankruptcies which were declared by the court fourteen or more years before the date of the credit report.
- Unpaid judgments which were declared by the court ten or more years before the date of the credit report.
- Paid tax liens which were paid seven or more years before the date of the credit report.
- Paid judgments which were declared by the court seven or more years before the date of the credit report.
- Suits which were filed against you seven or more years before the date of the credit report.
- Accounts which were placed for collection or charged to profit and loss seven or more years before the date of the credit report.
- Records of arrest, indictment information, misdemeanor complaint or the conviction of a crime in which the date of disposition, release or parole precede the credit report by seven or more years. A conviction no longer must be reported if a full pardon was granted for it, nor must an arrest, indictment, information or misdemeanor complaint be reported if a conviction did not result from it.
- Unlawful detainer actions where the person against whom the action was filed won.
- Any other information that will hurt your chances of getting credit, if the event occurred seven years or more before the date of the credit report.

The credit reporting agency may report any of the above items if it is giving a report for:

- A credit transaction which involves $50,000 or more.
- A life insurance transaction which involves $100,000 or more.
- The possibility of employment of a person at a salary of $30,000 or more.
- The rental of a dwelling unit which exceeds $1,000 per month.

As previously explained, you can change inaccurate or misleading information and request that the bureau send either the corrected information or your statement to anyone who requested a credit check during the past six months.

You may have legal remedies if you were illegally denied credit. If, after reviewing your credit file, you believe you were denied credit merely because of your sex or marital status or the other grounds described in this chapter, and you have reason to believe that a man with the same assets and credit history as you would receive credit, you may wish to get legal assistance. There are several government agencies you may contact about certain types of credit discrimination. The names and addresses of these agencies can be found in the directory at the back of this book. You may also wish to contact a private attorney about the possibility of recovering actual and punitive damages.

CANCELLATION OF CREDIT CARDS: A credit card issuer must give you notice of cancellation of your credit card. Unless requested by the cardholder, no card issuer can cancel a credit card without having first given the cardholder thirty-days written notice of its intention to do so unless:

- Within the past ninety days the cardholder has been in violation of the provision of his or her agreement with the card issuer, or
- The card issuer has evidence or a reasonable belief that the cardholder is unwilling or unable to repay his or her obligations or that an unauthorized use of the card may be made.

CREDIT CARD THEFT: A cardholder may be liable for the unauthorized use of a credit card only if all the following conditions are met:

- The card is an accepted credit card.
- The liability is not more than $50.
- The card issuer gives adequate notice to the cardholder of the potential liability.
- The card issuer has provided the cardholder with a description of the means by which the issuer may be notified of loss or theft of the card.
- The unauthorized use occurs before the card issuer has been notified that an unauthorized use of the credit card has occurred or may occur as a result of the loss, theft or otherwise misuse of the card.

Always read the information concerning lost of stolen credit cards that is mailed to you when you receive your cards.

If you are aware of credit practices by a store or agency that clearly violate the laws described in this book, you should send your written complaint to your local State Attorney General's Office.

BILL COLLECTORS AND COLLECTION AGENCIES

Bill collecting is big business, and just like any other business, the idea is to make as much money as possible. How you should respond to bill collectors depends upon what you want from them. You already know what they want. You may want or need extra time to pay your bills, or reduce the amount of your payment, or you may wish not to pay the bill at all. Whatever you want, you must remember that bill collectors work on the psychology of fear. If they have intimidated you, as they do most people, they have won, and will make a profit like any other business.

Everyone has to deal with bill collectors at one time or another. Collection agencies, through their letters and bill collectors, while on the telephone or in person, can be extremely intimidating to people unaware of their rights. In this section you will discover that there really is not much a collection agency can do to you. You must decide your best course of action and be firm about it. If you stay within your rights and do not panic, you will be able to take the necessary steps to take care of your debts and your peace of mind.

CAN'T PAY THE BILLS: You will receive a form letter, usually generated by a computer, notifying you when a payment is late on any bill. The computer, in effect, holds a package of notices and sends out one notice after another, waiting a certain period of time between mailings. Each notice is a little more threatening than the last, until finally you will be informed that if you do not pay immediately, your account will be turned over to an attorney for legal actions. Normally this is not true, as lawyers' fees would not justify the cost to recover the sums usually owed. The creditor will give the account to a collection agency and it will take at least several months to start a lawsuit.

Collection notices vary in content from company to company. Some remind you of your valuable credit rating. While other notices spend more effort convincing you of the pending lawsuit, wage attachments and repossession policies that are soon to follow. Many companies will contact you by telephone one or more times to ask you when they can expect a payment. Many large companies, such as department stores, other retailers and gasoline companies, have their own small collection departments. These departments typically send the first few letters that are usually only reminders that you are late paying your bill. These companies realize very little out-of-pocket losses due to favorable tax laws which allow the company to deduct the value of the merchandise from their income. After several letters and a telephone call or two, your credit privileges will be canceled and the account will be turned over to a collection agency.

If you are temporarily short of funds and need only an extension of time in order to pay the bill, ask for it. Write a letter to explain the situation directly and politely. If you can send a partial payment of as little as $10 or $20, it will help your cause, but it is not absolutely necessary. This approach works better with the original creditor than it does once the bill has been turned over to a collection agency.

If you fail to pacify the creditor or believe that circumstances require a little more clout, you might consider contacting a lawyer and having him or her write the letter. The letter will say the same as yours would have, but the stationery alone will guarantee that more respect is given the request letter. The creditor knows that if he doesn't cooperate with the lawyer's request for more time, the lawyer is likely to recommend bankruptcy.

Sometimes companies will pretend to be a collection agency. They simply buy forms and stamps with a phony collection agency name on the letterhead and send them out themselves. You can verify a collection agency by looking them up in the telephone book. Some collection agencies offer creditors a series of letters with little or no other collection activity except listing the debtor as a bad credit risk. This is often used for small bills such as magazine subscriptions, doctor bills, etc. because the amount owed is too small to justify an expensive lawsuit and people will sometimes pay bills if they receive a series of letters.

You should set priorities for your house payment, car, food, electric, and gas bills, and pay these bills first, before paying any creditors not on your list or those at the very bottom of the priority list. Do not let bill collectors intimidate you into deviating from your payment plan.

HOW COLLECTION AGENCIES OPERATE: Eventually, most unpaid bills, whatever the source, are turned over to collection agencies. Most people in collection agencies are paid to be nasty. Occasionally you will find someone with compassion and understanding of your situation, but this is rare. Collection agencies receive a percentage of any recovered money, with the rest going back to the creditor. The percentage varies, usually on how easy the debt is to collect. Sometimes a collection agency will simply purchase old debts from the creditor and try to collect more than the price they paid for the debt, although this method is unusual.

Remember, collection agencies or other creditors cannot sue, take wages, harass you by mail or telephone, or otherwise harass you, if they cannot locate you. They usually will not spend time or make the necessary effort to locate you, especially for small debts of $100 to $300. Collection agencies use the information provided by the creditor, your address, telephone number, place of work, bank, car registration, etc. If you move, the agency will check with the post office for a forwarding address and will, of course, check with the telephone company for a new number or address. Should this fail, the next step will be to contact your place of employment. If you have changed jobs, the collector will claim to be a friend trying to contact you to get the address from a coworker or the personnel department. The last step is to contact the State Department of Motor Vehicles (DMV) to see if you have informed them of your new address. This information is available for $2 and collection agencies are, through the State Association of Collection Agencies, fighting all proposed legislation aimed at making DMV information confidential. Collection agencies may also check with the Registrar of Voters in your county or call neighbors to try to locate you.

When dealing with a collection agency located far from the creditor, you can gain time by raising several questions about the debt. You might question the accuracy of the balance claimed to be owed or state that you never received one of the items in question. This will slow down the collection process as all questions must be answered before the collection agency can proceed, which sometimes takes several months.

NEGOTIATING A SETTLEMENT: You should understand your situation, including the difference between your secured and unsecured debts. If you are working or have valuable property (such as land) that a creditor could seize, you should be particularly concerned to take defensive action before the collection agency can attach your assets. If you have not yet been sued and your auto and your home are not protected, contact a lawyer to discuss how to protect these assets. You have some time to negotiate your debt. Your wages, bank account and other property cannot be taken until after a judgment has been entered in court (tax obligations are an exception). This cannot occur until after you have been sued and have been served with legal papers.

Collection agencies commonly accept cash settlements far below the full amount of the debt to avoid spending months trying to collect the whole amount. There is no rule as to how much money they will accept, but one-third of the amount owed is a very good place to start your negotiation. Usually a settlement of forty to sixty percent of the debt is common. There is little incentive, however, for the agency to reduce the debt total if you offer payments. The possibility that you might stop paying after one or two payments is too great a risk for them to settle for anything less than cash, full payment or a lower negotiated amount.

When negotiating a cash settlement, you should paint a bleak picture of your financial circumstances and mention that you are aware that bankruptcy is always a possibility. You should also:

- Never tell a collection agency where you live, work, bank or can be reached if they don't already know.
- Never send in a payment by check from your bank. Use money orders and buy them at a place other than where you bank.
- Never contact a collection agency if you do not have the cash to negotiate a cash settlement.
- Never inform a collection agency if you are divorcing or separating. From the agency's perspective this weakens your negotiating position and establishes you as a high risk.

You may wish to have a lawyer help you negotiate your debt(s). Remember, a lawyer commands more respect than you do and has an intimidating affect on the collector. A lawyer mentioning the possibility of bankruptcy carries a lot more weight than if you mentioned it. Many states have laws prohibiting a collection agency from contacting you directly once they know you have retained a lawyer to handle the debt negotiation. If a collection agency does contact you after your lawyer has contacted the agency, you should contact the proper state agency at once.

NEGOTIATING ON SECURED DEBTS: A "secured debt" is a debt secured by an agreement stating that if the debt is not paid, the item used to secure the debt must be returned. The creditor or collector must get a judgment from the court if you do not return the item in question voluntarily. If, for instance, you secured a loan worth $1,600 with your living room furniture and the net worth of that furniture is now $350, you are better off voluntarily returning the furniture if the loan has a balance of $1,000. If you return the furniture, the debt is canceled. In the case of the furniture being worth as much or more than the $1,000 balance on the secured loan, the collector will be more willing to accept the furniture, although they would still prefer to have the money.

In the first case, you have the better negotiating position, and in the second, the collector has the better negotiating position, and you may find that you will have problems settling the debt easily.

HARASSMENT: Collection agencies make a living by harassing people. Often there is a fine line separating harassing conduct that is legal from that which is illegal. If you can catch the collection agency using an illegal tactic, you can often get the debt in question wiped out by knowing how to handle the situation.

A collection agency can contact you by mail or telephone and demand payment. In most states, you can stop a collection agency from communicating with you by simply telling them so in writing. After they have received your letter telling them not to contact you, legally they can only contact you to inform you that they are taking some specific action, such as filing papers in court or garnishing your wages.

In most states, a collection agency cannot legally do any of the following:

- Use obscene or profane language.
- Threaten to harm you or any family member or friend.
- Threaten to publish or actually publish your name as a person who does not pay bills.
- Contact you about a bill that you tell them you don't owe until they send you proof of the debt.
- Claim to be law enforcement officers of any kind or in any way suggest that they are connected with any federal,

state, county or local government. The exception is child support.

- Send you any written document that looks like a court form or government document.
- Repeatedly use the telephone to annoy you.
- Contact your employer, except to verify employment or, following a court order or your written approval, garnish wages to collect on a debt.
- Threaten to have welfare or unemployment benefits cut off.
- Call you at work if you or your employer tell them not to. If this becomes a problem, put your request in writing and keep a copy of the written request.
- Falsely pretend that you have committed a crime.
- Falsely pretend that a legal action is being started against you.
- Threaten to take your property unless they have a court judgment.
- Claim to be an attorney or use attorney's stationery when they are not.
- Falsely claim that the debt will be increased by the addition of attorney's fees, service fees, finance charges, etc.
- Falsely threaten to sue. The collector can be liable for your actual damages and for a fine.

You must keep all documents that shed light on your complaint and try, if possible, to have a friend listen in on any abusive oral conversations with the collection agency. You can, after complaining to the State and Federal Trade Commission, retain an attorney to represent you in a damage suit in either state or federal court (fees and court costs can be recovered if you win). You may be entitled to actual damages (including pain and suffering) and punitive damages. The collector may be imprisoned and/or fined. You can also write a letter explaining the violation to the original creditor with copies to collection agency, the state agency effected, your local state senator and assembly person and the Federal Trade Commission. If you persist and make enough of an issue out of it, you are likely to get the whole debt canceled in exchange for discontinuing your protest.

BUSINESS ESTABLISHMENTS

Women and men are entitled to equal treatment in business establishments. If you are denied entrance or services illegally by any business establishment, you may file a legal action against the business for damages and attorney's fees.

The U.S. Supreme Court recently upheld a New York City ordinance that outlaws sex discrimination in membership by most large private clubs.

By definition a "business establishment" is a place generally open to the public. Examples of business establishments include restaurants, bars, stores, movie theaters, hotels, motels, shopping centers, housing accommodations, apartment buildings and real estate brokers' and doctors' offices.

Not all clubs meet the legal definition of a business establishment. Some clubs that are supported by private membership and open only to members and their families may not be business establishments and may not be covered by this law. However, even a private club can become a business establishment and be subject to laws against discrimination to the extent that it permits public and business functions to occur on its premises.

A number of cities have local ordinances that outlaw discriminatory membership practices for most large private clubs. None of the local ordinances are exactly the same, and not all private clubs are covered. You may want to contact your city attorney to find out whether your city has such a local ordinance, and whether it is being challenged in court.

YOUR RIGHTS IN A BUSINESS ESTABLISHMENT: It is illegal for a business establishment to treat women less favorably than men entering and using the establishment. This means that you, as a woman, are allowed to enter any office, restaurant, bar or other business establishment on the same basis as any other person is allowed to enter. You must be given the same privileges, accommodations, goods and services as any other person coming into the place. For example, it is illegal for a restaurant to refuse to serve a woman seated alone if the restaurant will serve a man seated alone. It is illegal for a restaurant to refuse to serve you because you are gay.

Sex-based promotional discounts, such as women's day/night at the car wash or nightclubs, also constitute illegal sex-based discrimination. Business establishments must provide equal advantages and privileges to all customers "no matter what their sex."

It is illegal for nearly any business that has a state license for some activity to refuse to provide that licensed activity to you because you are a woman. For example, it is illegal for most establishments with a state liquor license to refuse to provide that licensed activity to you because you are a woman. The business can lose its license for such a refusal.

Rental housing is considered a business establishment. It is thus illegal for an apartment owner to refuse to rent an apartment to a woman merely because she is a woman. An apartment owner also cannot refuse to rent to you because you are a lesbian or because you have children.

A condominium owner may not discriminate in rentals or sales against people who have a child under eighteen years of age. However, senior citizen housing facilities are legally permitted.

LEGAL REMEDIES: If you believe you have been denied equal rights by a business establishment because of your gender, there are a number of possible remedies you may seek.

You may want to hire a private attorney. A private attorney may file an action in court to recover up to three times your actual damages, but not less than $250 in damages for each act of discrimination, and your attorney's fees.

If you have reason to believe that a business establishment has a continuing practice of denying equal rights because of sex, race, color, religion, ancestry, national origin or sexual orientation, you may notify the district attorney, city or county attorney or the state attorney general. These government agencies have the power to bring legal action to stop the business from future acts of discrimination.

CONTRACTS

A contract is an agreement between two or more people, usually to provide some goods or services or perform some action. It is illegal for a contract for goods or services to be discriminatory on the basis of sex, race, creed, color, nationality, ethnic origin or sexual preference. The laws that apply to making and enforcing contracts are technical and often require the services of a lawyer when disputes arise. However, it is important to have some knowledge about the basic elements of contracts.

A contract is an agreement that can be legally enforced. To have a contract, someone makes an offer, someone accepts that offer and there is "consideration." Consideration is any benefit that is given in exchange. A valid contract must also have a lawful "object," the thing that the person who receives the consideration promises to do or not to do.

The general rule is that an offer can be revoked or taken back until it is accepted. If you pay someone to keep an offer open for a period of time, an "option contract" is formed and the offer may not be revoked for a certain period of time. If someone makes an offer to you and promises not to take it back and you act because you relied on the offer, a contract is formed. Sometimes specific actions by parties can create "implied in fact contracts."

A contract may be written or verbal. Generally, both written and verbal contracts are binding and enforceable in a court of law. However, in many states, verbal contracts are not enforceable if they deal with more than a certain amount of money or are negotiated for a long period of time. You should, whenever possible, put all agreements in writing.

Before entering into any contract, a woman should know what guarantees and warranties are included in the agreement and what penalties will be lodged for violations of the contract. Be careful about the fine print. What is said and what is in writing may be two different things and, if signed, the written work becomes legal and binding. All contracts should also state under what circumstances they may be canceled.

CONTRACTS WITH SPECIFIC TYPES OF BUSINESSES: Many states have laws governing contracts with specific types of businesses. You should check with your local district attorney, lawyer or legal aid for laws or exceptions to the law for the specific type of business with which you are entering into a contract before agreeing to any specific terms or conditions within a contract.

MAIL ORDER GOODS: If you receive goods or services in the mail or delivered to your home that you did not order verbally or in writing, you do not need to pay for them. These goods become gifts to you under most state laws. You are under no obligation to pay for something you did not order.

If you receive unsolicited goods or services and the company that sent the goods tries to collect payment for the goods, you can go to court to stop the company from bothering you. If you win in court, you may also be awarded attorneys' fees. You may wish to report such collection tactics to your local district attorney or to the attorney general.

DOOR-TO-DOOR SALES: For your protection, federal law now permits the buyer of products or services which are sold in the home (including courses of instruction, but not including the services of real estate brokers, physicians, attorneys, security dealers or investment counselors, optometrists, dentists, certain financial services, insurance sales and mobile homes or goods sold with them, and most vehicles or goods sold with them) to cancel the contract if the following conditions exist:

- The contract is for more than $25. The law applies to cash sales as well as installment sales.
- The sale was made in the home or at any place that is not the seller's normal business office. The law applies even if the buyer signs in his or her home but the seller signs the contract later in his or her office.

If you sign a contract you made with a door-to-door salesperson, you have three days to cancel the contract without obligation. Sundays and holidays are not counted in the three days. The contract has to explain all of this, and there must be a cancellation form attached to the contract that you can tear off and send in. The sales person must write on that form the date of the contract and the date by which you must cancel. The salesperson must also tell you of your right to cancel.

If you cancel a door-to-door contract, the company must return all of your down payment and can make no charge for the cancellation. You must, of course, be willing to give back the goods if you have received any. However, the seller is not responsible for collecting the goods, and if the seller fails to pick up the goods in twenty days, you may keep them.

Warning: Be cautious about giving money in advance to a door-to-door salesperson. You may never see him or her again, and the "company" may be difficult to find. Most states require that the salesperson carries state-issued identification. You should request this identification and verify its authenticity before purchasing.

INSURANCE

There are many types of insurance that provide valuable protection against accidents, illness, unemployment and for survivors of deceased persons. In this section, five types of insurance are described:

- MEDICAL
- DISABILITY
- AUTOMOBILE
- LIFE
- STATE UNEMPLOYMENT INSURANCE.

For each type of insurance, there is a description of the general protection given, types of benefits paid and equal rights under insurance laws.

Insurance law is a complicated subject. For specific questions about your own policies, you should contact your insurance agent or the State Department of Insurance in your state.

No insurer is allowed to refuse to issue any contract of insurance or to cancel or decline to renew such insurance because of the sex, marital status or sexual orientation of the insured or prospective insured.

MEDICAL INSURANCE: Medical insurance pays all or part of your hospital and doctor bills when you are sick or injured. You may have an individual policy, a group policy through your employer, or you may be eligible for a state health care plan. Private and public employers are required to give covered employees notice before their medical, surgical or hospital benefits are discontinued. Health insurance is a very complicated field. If you have any major problems or concerns related to your health insurance, it would be wise for you to contact a private attorney.

MEDICAL INSURANCE FOR WOMEN: Medical insurance policies must have the same waiting periods for men as for women. However, a medical insurance policy, unless contained in an employee fringe benefit plan, may impose some minimum waiting period after the insurance coverage begins before the policy will pay for your pregnancy.

If your employer's group plan covers the wives of male workers, it must cover the husbands of female workers. Likewise, a medical insurance policy must provide coverage for the children of female employees, if it provides coverage for the children of male employees. And, medical insurance policies can ask women to have medical check-ups only if men are also asked to have them.

Medical insurance policies that include coverage for mastectomy and prosthetic devices and reconstructive surgery incident to mastectomy must provide coverage for mammography.

MEDICAL INSURANCE AND PREGNANCY: Where an employer of fifteen or more employees offers medical coverage to his or her employees, he or she is required to cover pregnancy and related medical conditions to the same extent that other medical conditions are covered (except that an employer plan does not have to pay for an abortion unless the life of the mother would be endangered if the fetus were carried to term or unless medical complications have arisen from an abortion).

The medical insurance policy must provide the same pregnancy coverage for unmarried employees as it does for married employees.

Some states allow for women to collect disability benefits from the state for absences due to pregnancy if a doctor certifies that she is disabled. Such benefits may last for the same period allowed for any other disability. For information about pregnancy disability, contact the State Disability Insurance Office or the State Employment Development Department nearest you.

Employers may not exclude pregnancy from coverage under employee group, private disability insurance plans. Disability due to pregnancy must be treated the same as any other disability. If employers not covered by Title V11 provide more than six weeks for accrued leave for disability to temporarily disabled employees, they are required to provide at least six weeks of disability leave for pregnancy, childbirth or related medical conditions. Any employer who provides less than four months leave for temporarily disabled employees must provide up to four months leave to an employee disabled by pregnancy, childbirth or related medical conditions.

A medical insurance policy, unless it is part of an employee fringe benefit plan, will cover genetic testing in cases of high risk pregnancy, if agreed upon by the insurer and the policyholder. Prospective policyholders must be informed of the availability of such coverage.

You may not collect state unemployment payments if you left your job solely because you are pregnant. You can collect state unemployment payments after the birth of your child or at the end of your pregnancy if you are able to work and your previous job has benefits. You may also be able to collect payments if you leave employment to accompany your spouse or someone to whom marriage is imminent to a place from which it is impractical to commute and to which a transfer is not available.

It is illegal for you to be forced to leave your job because you are pregnant, unless, in the opinion of your doctor or other licensed health care practitioner, you are unable to perform the essential duties of the job or to perform these duties without undue risk to yourself or other persons. Neither company policy nor a union collective bargaining agreement may require you to leave your job solely because you are pregnant.

Individual medical insurance policies must not exclude coverage for complications of pregnancy. In addition, individual medical insurance policies cannot exclude payments for disorders of the reproductive organs.

An application for private disability insurance can ask questions about female sexual organs and disorders without asking similar questions of male applicants. However, most applications inquire into the fertility-related medical history of all applicants.

STERILIZATION: If a disability insurance policy or self-insured employee welfare benefit plan pays for sterilization, it cannot place an exclusion, limitation or reduction on such benefit based on the reason for requesting the sterilization.

PRIVATE DISABILITY INSURANCE: Private disability insurance pays you money to make up for wages lost when you are unable to work because of sickness or injury. Men and women in the same job must be offered the same private disability insurance coverage, and benefits from private disability insurance must cover the same time period for women and men.

If a policy provides coverage for work men do at home or for a relative, then it must provide coverage for the same work done by women at home or for a relative, except for coverage for homemaking, which insurance companies do not have to provide for either gender.

Every disability insurance policy that includes coverage for mastectomy must provide coverage for mammography.

A disability insurance company cannot discriminate against a person carrying a gene that, under certain circumstances, may be associated with a disability in that person's offspring but not in them, such as Tay-Sachs disease, sickle-cell anemia or hemophilia.

A disability insurance company cannot refuse to insure or to charge a different rate to a person with a physical or mental impairment unless to do so is based on sound actuarial principles, or is related to actual and reasonably anticipated experience.

AUTOMOBILE INSURANCE: Before you buy or even drive a car, you should obtain car insurance unless you qualify for other forms of financial responsibility allowed by law.

Insurance, required by the laws of most states, covers injuries to yourself and your passengers and injuries to the drivers and passengers of the other cars if you are in an accident. If the accident is your fault, these bills, as well as the bills for property damage, can be extremely high. Some car insurance policies also pay for damages to your car due to an accident or vandalism.

Automobile insurance rates have been based on your age, sex, driving record and other factors. State laws vary, therefore, you should contact an insurance agent or state agency to determine the laws in your state.

An auto insurance company may charge you a rate based on your husband's driving record or it may charge you premiums based on the driving records of other members of your household, even if the policy is in your name. In addition, an auto insurance company may insist on writing a policy for your entire household rather than for you as an individual.

LIFE INSURANCE: Life insurance is money intended to provide for your husband and children (or other family members or friends) should you die.

The present statutory laws of most states allow a life insurance company to charge men and women different rates for life insurance. This may vary from state to state; you should contact an insurance agent or state agency to check the laws of your state. Life insurance companies use statistics on how long people are expected to live (these statistics are called "actuarial tables") to calculate different insurance rates for men and women. Women are usually expected to live longer, so their life insurance policy rates are usually lower. However, it is the opinion of many state attorney generals that gender-based differentials in the contracting of life insurance and life annuities may violate the equal protection clause of the U.S. Constitution. This issue has yet to be ruled on by the courts.

If a life insurance company insures men with a particular type of job, it must insure women with the same type of job. In addition, if a life insurance company asks for a physical examination as a precondition to insurance, it must require the exam of both men and women.

A life insurance company cannot discriminate against a person carrying a gene that, under certain circumstances, may be associated with a disability in that person's offspring but not in them, such as Tay-Sachs disease, sickle-cell anemia or hemophilia.

A life insurance company cannot refuse to insure or charge a different rate to a person with a physical or mental impairment unless to do so is based on sound actuarial principles or is related to actual and reasonably anticipated experience.

UNEMPLOYMENT INSURANCE BENEFITS: Currently, unemployment insurance benefits are paid through federal extensions because of an unusually high unemployment rate. The standard benefit is twenty-six weeks. You are eligible if:

- You are out of work because you were laid off through no fault of your own, because you were fired for something other than misconduct or because you quit for good cause and,
- You are able to work, are actively seeking employment and have been unemployed for a waiting period of one week and,
- You earned at least $1,200 from unemployment insurance benefits that covered an employer during the "base period." (The base period is the one-year period calculated from the filing date of the unemployment insurance claim.) or

- You earned at least $900 while working a minimum of eight weeks, during which time you earned at least $20 per week.

If a woman is unable to work due to pregnancy disability, she may collect disability benefits for absences due to pregnancy, if a doctor specifies that she was disabled. Pregnancy-related disability benefits are generally paid for a total of six weeks.

If you believe that you have been refused insurance or have been treated differently because you are a woman or because of your marital status, you may wish to contact the State Department of Insurance, Consumer Services Bureau or the Equal Employment Opportunity Commission.

PUBLIC ASSISTANCE

Public assistance programs that provide money and other benefits to needy persons are listed below. If you believe that you qualify for any of these benefits, you may contact the agencies listed in the directory at the end of this book for information about programs that may apply to you.

FOOD STAMPS

Food stamps are vouchers that you can exchange for food. You no longer have to pay money for food stamps. The amount of food stamps for which you are eligible is calculated according to the number of persons in the household. The monetary amount changes each October.

ELIGIBILITY: You are eligible for food stamps if:
- Your maximum gross income, which is all income earned and unearned, including any form of public assistance, does not exceed a certain amount per month per person in the household (these figures change annually).
- Your maximum adjusted income (net) is no greater than a certain amount per month per person (these figures change annually).

- You have no more than a certain amount in resources (for one person).
- You are registered to work.

If you are elderly or disabled and live in a separate household, you are eligible if your maximum gross income is no greater than a certain amount per person. You must be a resident of the United States and either a citizen or an alien lawfully admitted to permanent residence as an immigrant to be eligible for food stamps.

Discrimination is prohibited. State and federal laws prohibit discrimination against any household by reason of race, color, religion, creed, national origin, sex, marital status or political belief to the extent not in conflict with federal law in determining your eligibility for food stamps.

TO FIGURE YOUR ADJUSTED INCOME: To determine your adjusted income, first take your monthly income, then subtract the following amounts (deductions):

- Generally, a food stamp household can deduct twenty percent of its earnings from work.
- A standard deduction of a set amount. This amount will be increased every October by a cost of living factor.
- Dependent care costs, if you pay them, so someone in the household can earn up to a certain amount.
- Shelter costs (rent, mortgage, utilities, basic telephone, etc.).

These costs may not exceed a certain amount per month in forty-eight states.

A household with a member who is sixty or older, or who gets social security because he or she is disabled, can deduct the medical expenses of that person over a specified amount each month. Those households can also deduct unlimited shelter costs as opposed to other households, which are limited to a maximum deduction.

Women residing in a shelter for battered women may qualify for food stamps if they prepare their own food and meet the other criteria listed here.

EXPEDITED ASSISTANCE For information and assistance with regard to food stamps, please call your County Social Services Department and ask to speak with staff who work for the food stamp program.

AID TO FAMILIES WITH DEPENDENT CHILDREN

AFDC provides money and services to needy families with children until the families can become self-supporting. AFDC is governed by federal and state laws, but the program is run by your County Welfare Department.

ELIGIBILITY: You are eligible if you are a single parent or pregnant woman in "need." You are also eligible if you are single, with at least one child under eighteen, in "need" and with "child deprivation." Eighteen-year-old children may be eligible if they will graduate from high school or the equivalent level of vocational technical training on a full-time basis before their nineteenth birthday.

Need is based on your income and personal assets. Child deprivation means that one parent is absent from the home, disabled, deceased or unemployed or working less than 100 hours per month. Mothers as well as fathers can be considered unemployed parents under the AFDC program. In addition, if you qualify for AFDC, you may also qualify for food stamps.

BENEFITS: Maximum benefits for AFDC are adjusted annually in July to reflect costs-of-living increases and are expressed in terms of maximum amounts per persons in the household.

All recipients of AFDC, except for single parents with children under six, are required to sign up for the Greater Avenues to Independence program (GAIN). GAIN will assist you in finding a job. Services offered through GAIN include job training, and financial assistance for education and child care.

To apply for AFDC benefits, call your County Social Services Department and ask for the Aid to Families with Dependent Children Program.

SUPPLEMENTAL SECURITY INCOME

Supplemental Security Income (SSI) is a federal program that provides financial assistance to needy people who are over sixty-five, blind or disabled.

ELIGIBILITY: You are eligible for SSI if you:
- Are a U.S. citizen or permanent resident.
- Are over sixty-five or disabled or blind.
- Have limited income and limited resources.

BENEFITS: The maximum SSI benefits are set forth in section 12200 of the welfare and institutions code and are subject to annual cost-of-living increases in January of each year. However, if you are living in the household of another and receiving room and board in-kind, your benefits will be lower than those set forth in section 12200.

If you are eligible for the above benefits, you will also receive a Medicaid card that entitles you to many free medical services.

If you are living where you cannot prepare your own meals, you are entitled to an extra allowance.

If you are living in a non-medical boarding care facility, the basic benefit is a certain amount per month. Additionally, you are entitled to a minimum amount for your personal needs not provided by the facility out of this first amount.

To apply for SSI benefits, call the Social Security Administration of the U.S. Department of Health and Human Services and ask for the Supplemental Security Income program.

STATE DISABILITY INSURANCE

State disability insurance payments may be available to you. For best results, you should contact a private attorney or legal aid to determine your eligibility.

ELIGIBILITY: You are usually eligible for state disability insurance (SDI) if you:

- Are suffering a loss of wages as a result of a disability.
- Have a doctor's certificate that you are unable to do "regular and customary" work.
- Were not injured on the job; and
- Have been paid wages of a certain minimum amount by your employer.

If you were injured on the job, you may be eligible for worker's compensation.

BENEFITS: Benefits from SDI are paid for a maximum of fifty-two weeks. To apply for SDI benefits, call the Employment Development Department office nearest you and ask about disability insurance claims.

WOMEN, INFANTS AND CHILDREN

Good nutrition, including foods rich in protein, calcium, iron, vitamins A, C, and D, is very important during a child's growth and development. The Special Supplemental Food program for Women, Infants and Children (WIC) is a federally funded program that provides nutritious food supplements and nutrition counseling to pregnant and nursing women and to infants and children who are five years old or younger. You may qualify for this program if you are in need because of low income and have nutrition-related health problems. The food supplements include iron-fortified formula, fortified milk and cheese, eggs, iron-rich cereals and fruit juices.

For more information about WIC programs in your area, you may want to contact the Department of Health Services WIC Supplemental Food Section.

GENERAL ASSISTANCE

There are other social service benefits available. What benefits are available and the requirements for receiving them very from county to county. Call your county Social Services Department and ask for the General Assistance Program.

CHAPTER 3

SOCIAL SECURITY

If you're like most people, you tend to think of Social Security simply as a retirement program. Although it's true that most of the beneficiaries (about sixty percent) receive retirement benefits, many others get Social Security because they are disabled, a dependent of someone who gets Social Security or a widow.

Depending on your circumstances, you may be eligible for Social Security at any age. More than forty million people, almost one-out-of-six Americans, collect some kind of Social Security benefit.

Social Security is not intended to be your only source of income. Instead, it is meant to be used to supplement the pensions, insurance, savings and other investments you will accumulate during your working years.

SOCIAL SECURITY NUMBER

Your Social Security number is used to track your earnings while you are working and to track your benefits once you are getting Social Security. Almost everyone has a Social Security number, as the Internal Revenue Service requires that a Social Security number be shown on tax returns for all dependents age one and older. In most states, the Social Security number application process is a part of the birth registration procedure, and this is usually taken care of before the mother and child leave the hospital.

CARD REPLACEMENT: If you need a Social Security number, if you lost your card and need another one or if you need to change your name on your current card, call or visit a Social Security Office. You will be asked to fill out an application form. You will need certain documents depending on your situation and all documents must be originals or certified copies. You will need:

- A birth certificate and some other form of identification for a new card.
- Some form of identification for a replacement card.
- A marriage certificate or divorce papers for a name change.

SOCIAL SECURITY TAXES

Social Security taxes are used to pay for all Social Security benefits. In addition, a portion of your taxes is used to pay for part of your Medicare coverage. General tax revenues, not Social Security taxes, are used to finance the Supplemental Security Income (SSI) program.

If you work for someone else, you and your employer each pay 7.65 percent of your gross salary, up to a limit determined by congress. In 1993, the limit was $57,600. This is the "FICA" deduction you will see on your paycheck.

If you are self-employed, you pay 15.3 percent of your taxable income into Social Security, up to the limit of $57,600. However, there are special deductions you can take when you file your tax return that are intended to offset your tax rate. (See Publication No. 05-10022 for further information.)

EXTRA TAXES FOR MEDICARE

If you made more than $57,600 in 1993, you continue to pay the Medicare portion of the Social Security tax up to a limit of $135,000. The Medicare portion of the tax is 1.45 percent for employers and employees each, and 2.9 percent for self-employed persons.

ELIGIBILITY "CREDITS"

As you work and pay taxes, you earn Social Security "credits." Almost everyone who works earns four credits per year; you earn one credit for each $590 in earnings you have up to a maximum of four credits per year. (The amount of money needed to earn one credit goes up every year.) How many credits you need to qualify for Social Security depends on your age and the kind of benefits for which you might be eligible. Most people need forty credits (ten years of work) to qualify for benefits. Younger people need fewer credits to be eligible for disability benefits or for their family members to be eligible for survivors' benefits if they should die. (See Publication No.'s 05-10035, 05-10084, 05-10029.)

YOUR BENEFIT

The amount of your Social Security benefit is based on factors such as your date of birth, the type of benefit for which you are applying and, most importantly, your earnings. To receive a detailed, personal estimate of your Social Security retirement, disability and survivors' benefit, you need to call or visit a Social Security Office and ask for it. You will be issued a Personal Earnings and Benefit Estimate Statement.

In general, your benefit is based on your earnings averaged over most of your working lifetime. In its simplest terms, your benefit is figured according to the following formula:

- Figure the number of years of your earnings to use as a base;

NOTE: Retirement benefits: for everybody born after 1928 and retiring in 1991 or later, the number is thirty-five years. Fewer years are used for people born in 1928 or earlier. Disability and survivors' benefits use most of the years of earnings posted to your spouse's record.

- Adjust the earnings for inflation;
- Determine the average adjusted monthly earnings based on the number of years figured; and then
- Multiply the average adjusted earnings by percentages in a formula specified by law.

The formula results in benefits that replace about forty-two percent of a person's earnings. This applies to people who had average earnings during their working years. The percentage is lower for people in the upper income brackets and higher for people with low incomes. (That is because the Social Security benefits formula is weighted in favor of low income workers who have less opportunity to save and invest during their working years.)

If you haven't worked long enough to get Social Security or if you get only a small amount, you may be eligible for Supplemental Security Income (SSI).

To apply for benefits you must file a claim at any Social Security Office. It is best to call ahead for an appointment at (800) 772-1213.

The following is a list of some of the documents you may need when you sign up for Social Security:

- Your Social Security card (or a record of your number).
- Your birth certificate.
- Children's birth certificates (if they are applying).
- Marriage certificate (if signing up on a spouse's record).
- Your most recent W-2 form or your tax return if you are self-employed.

Additional documents may be required. When you sign up for benefits, they will let you know if other documents are needed. If you don't have all the documents needed, you can still sign up for benefits and someone at the Social Security Office will help you gather the information you need.

You may have your benefits either deposited directly into your bank account or come to you in the mail. If you choose direct deposit, have your bank account numbers with you when you sign up.

FULL RETIREMENT: If you were born before 1938, you will be eligible for your full Social Security benefit at age sixty-five. However, beginning in the year 2000, the age at which full benefits are payable will increase in gradual steps from ages sixty-five to sixty-seven. This affects people born in 1938 and later. If you were born in 1940, your full retirement age is sixty-five and six months. If you were born in 1950, your full retirement age is sixty-six. Anyone born in 1960 or later will be eligible for full retirement benefits at age sixty-seven.

REDUCED BENEFITS: No matter what your full retirement age is, you may start receiving benefits as early as sixty-two. However, if you start your benefits early, they are reduced 5/9 of one percent for each month before your full retirement age.

There are disadvantages and advantages to taking your benefits before your full retirement age. The disadvantage is that your benefits are permanently reduced. The advantage is that you collect benefits for a longer period of time. Each person's situation is different, so make sure you carefully analyze your own situation and possibly consult with an accountant before you decide to retire.

LATE RETIREMENT: Some people continue to work full time beyond their full retirement age and they do not sign up for Social Security until later. This delay in retirement can increase your benefits in two ways:

- Your extra income usually will increase your average earnings, and the higher your average earnings, the higher your benefits will be.
- A special credit is given to people who delay retirement. This credit, which is a percentage added to your benefits, varies depending on your date of birth. For people who turned sixty-five in 1993, the rate was four percent per year. That rate gradually increases in future years, until it reaches eight percent per year for people turning sixty-five in the year 2008 or later.

DISABILITY BENEFITS: If you have earned enough Social Security "credits" on your own work record, you may qualify for disability benefits. However it is important to note that other kinds of disability benefits are available from Social Security, depending on your circumstances. (See Publication No. 05-10029.) These include:

- Widows and widowers with disabilities who are eligible for benefits on the record of a spouse.
- People with disabilities who have low income and few assets who might be eligible for SSI benefits.
- Children over age eighteen with disabilities who might be eligible for Social Security benefits on the record of a par-

ent, or children of any age with disabilities who might be eligible for SSI benefits on their own. (See Publication No. 05-10026.)

A disability is a physical or mental impairment that is expected to keep you from doing any "substantial" work for at least a year. Generally, monthly earnings of $500 or more are considered substantial. Or you must have a condition that is expected to result in your death. Social Security is not intended for a temporary condition or partial disability.

If you become disabled, you should file for disability benefits as soon as possible. You can shorten the time it takes to process your claim if you have the following medical and vocational information when you apply:

- The names, addresses and telephone numbers of your doctors, and of hospitals, clinics, etc., where you have been treated.
- A summary of where you worked in the past fifteen years and the kind of work you did.

Because Social Security disability rules are different from those of other private plans or government agencies, you may qualify for disability from some other agency and still not be eligible for Social Security disability. Further, having a statement from your doctor indicating you are disabled does not mean you will be automatically eligible for Social Security disability payments.

IF YOU HAVE HIV INFECTION: Acquired immunodeficiency syndrome (AIDS) is caused by the virus HIV. Generally speaking, people with HIV infection fall into two broad categories:

- Those with symptomatic HIV infection, including AIDS.
- Those with HIV infection but no symptoms.

People with HIV infection are receiving Social Security or SSI disability benefits. You may be eligible even if your condition improves or stabilizes enough for you to return to work. Social Security is committed to helping all people with HIV infection. (See Publication No. 05-10020.)

Your monthly disability benefits, in most cases, will begin with the sixth month of your disability. Do not delay signing up for Social Security benefits because of this "waiting period." By filing early, all the paperwork will be processed before your first check is due. There is no waiting period for disabled children's benefits or for SSI disability payments.

If you are getting workers' compensation or certain other government disability benefits, your Social Security disability benefits may be reduced, or the fact that you get Social Security may reduce your other payments. This is because the sum of all disability payments to you and your family cannot exceed eighty percent of your earnings averaged over a period of time shortly before you became disabled.

You will continue to get disability benefits unless your condition improves or you return to "substantial" work. Your claim will be checked periodically to determine your disability status. You may be required to undergo a special test or medical examination.

There are special rules that help people who would like to return to work but are concerned about the effect this might have on their disability benefits. These rules offer special incentives that permit people to try working without the risk of a sudden loss of their monthly benefits and their Medicare coverage. (See Publication No. 05-10095.)

BENEFITS FOR THE FAMILY: When you start collecting Social Security retirement or disability benefits, other members of your family might also be eligible for payments. For example, benefits can be paid to:

- Your spouse, if he or she is sixty-two or older (unless he or she collects a higher Social Security benefit on his or her own record).
- Your spouse at any age if he or she is caring for your child (the child must be under sixteen or disabled and receiving Social Security benefits).
- Your children, if they are unmarried and under eighteen; under nineteen but in elementary or secondary school as a

full-time student; or eighteen or older and severely disabled (the disability must have started before age twenty-two).

Usually, a family member will be eligible for a monthly benefit that is up to fifty percent of your retirement or disability rate, depending on how many family members are eligible. Your spouse is eligible for a share of the fifty percent rate if he or she is sixty-five or older, or if he or she is caring for your minor or disabled child. If your spouse is under sixty-five and is not caring for a minor or disabled child, the rate is reduced by a small percentage for each month before age sixty-five. Currently, the lowest reduced benefit is 37.5 percent at age sixty-two.

There is a limit to the amount of money that can be paid on each Social Security record. The limit varies, but is generally equal to about 150 to 180 percent of your retirement benefit. (It may be less for disability benefits.) If the sum of the benefits payable on your account is greater than this family limit, then the benefits to the family members will be reduced proportionately. Your benefits will not be affected.

DIVORCED PERSONS: If you are divorced (even if you have remarried), your ex-spouse can be eligible for benefits on your record. In some situations, he or she could get benefits even if you are not receiving them. In order to qualify, your ex-spouse must:

- Have been married to you for at least ten years.
- Be at least sixty-two years old.
- Be unmarried.
- Not be eligible for an equal or higher benefit on his or her own Social Security record or on someone else's Social Security record.

If your ex-spouse receives benefits on your account, it does not affect the amount of any benefits payable to you or your other family members.

SURVIVORS' BENEFITS: When you die, certain members of your family may be eligible for benefits on your Social Security record if you had earned enough credits while you were working. The family members who can collect benefits include:

- A widow or widower who is sixty or older.
- A widow or widower who is fifty or older and disabled.
- A widow or widower at any age if she or he is caring for a child under sixteen or a disabled child who is receiving Social Security benefits.
- Children if they are unmarried and under eighteen; under nineteen but in an elementary or secondary school as a full-time student; or eighteen or older and severely disabled (the disability must have started before age twenty-two).
- Your parents, if they were dependent on you for at least half of their support.

The amount payable to your survivors is a percentage of your basic Social Security benefit—usually in a range from seventy-five to one hundred percent. The Personal Earnings and Benefit Estimate statement will provide you with a more accurate measurement of potential survivors' benefits payable on your record. Contact your local Social Security Office or call (800) 772-1213 to obtain a copy of your Personal Earnings and Benefit Estimate Statement.

SPECIAL ONE-TIME DEATH BENEFIT: If you had enough credits, a special one-time payment of $225 also will be made. This payment is made only to your spouse or minor children.

DIVORCED WIDOWS AND WIDOWERS: If you are divorced (even if you have remarried), your ex-spouse will be eligible for benefits on your record when you die. In order to qualify your ex-spouse must:

- Be at least sixty years old (or fifty if disabled) and have been married to you for at least ten years.
- Be any age if caring for a child who is eligible for benefits on your record.

- Not be eligible for an equal or higher benefit on his or her own record.
- Not be currently married, unless the remarriage occurred after age sixty or age fifty for disabled widows (in cases of remarriage after the age of sixty, your ex-spouse will be eligible for a widow's benefit on your record or a dependent's benefit on the record of his or her new spouse, whichever is higher.

If your ex-spouse receives benefits on your account, it does not affect the amount of any benefits payable to other survivors on your record.

RETIREMENT BENEFITS FOR WIDOW(ER)S: If you are receiving widow's or widower's (including divorced widow's or widower's) benefits, you should remember that you can switch to your own retirement benefits (assuming you are eligible and your retirement rate is higher than your widow's rate) as early as age sixty-two. In many cases, a widow(er) can begin receiving one benefit at a reduced rate and then switch to the other benefit at an unreduced rate at age sixty-five. The rules are complicated and vary depending on your situation, so you should talk to a Social Security representative about the options available to you.

MAXIMUM FAMILY BENEFITS: Like payments to your family members if you are retired or disabled, there is a limit to the amount of money that can be paid each month to your survivors. The limit varies, but is generally equal to about 150 to 180 percent of your benefit rate. If the sum of the benefits payable to your surviving family members is greater than this limit, then the benefits to your family will be reduced proportionately.

SUPPLEMENTAL SECURITY INCOME

This section provides a brief overview of the Supplemental Security Income (SSI) program. (See Publication No. 05-11000.) Supplemental Security Income is usually called "SSI" for short. Although this program is run by the Social Security Office, the money to pay for SSI benefits does not come from Social Security taxes or Social Security trust funds. SSI payments are financed by the general revenue funds of the U.S. Treasury.

SSI makes monthly payments to people who have low incomes and few assets. In addition, to get SSI you must:

- Be living in the United States or the Northern Mariana Islands.
- Be a U.S. citizen or be living in the United States legally.
- And you must be sixty-five or older, or blind, or disabled.

Children as well as adults can get SSI benefits because of blindness or disability.

To get SSI, your income and the value of the things you own must be below certain limits. The term "income," means the money you have coming in such as earnings, Social Security payments, or other government checks, pensions, etc. including "non-cash" items you receive such as the value of free food and shelter. How much income you can have and still be able to get SSI depends on whether you work or not and in which state you live. Although there is a basic national SSI payment rate, some states add money to the national payment, so they have higher SSI rates and higher income limits than other states. Check with your local Social Security office to find what the SSI rates and income limits are in your state.

"Assets" are the things you own such as property, cash and bank accounts. Not everything you own is counted when deciding whether you qualify for SSI benefits. For example, your home and many of your personal belongings are not counted and usually neither is your car.

You may be able to get SSI if the things you own that are counted are no more than $2,000 for one person, or $3,000 for a couple. Unlike the income category, these limits do not change from state to state.

SSI PAYMENTS: How much you will get from SSI depends on your other income and where you live. The basic monthly SSI check is the same in all states — $434 for one person and $652 for a couple. Some states add money to the basic rate, so you may get more if you live in one of these states. You will get less if you have other income.

SSI AND DISABILITIES: People with disabilities, including children, can get SSI if their income and assets are below the limits discussed in the previous sections. Most of the rules used to decide if a person has a condition severe enough to qualify for Social Security disability benefits also apply to SSI. The SSI program has special plans designed to help people who want to try to go back to work without the risk of suddenly losing their benefits or Medicaid coverage. (See Publication No. 05-10095 for this type of information. For special information about benefits for children with disabilities, see Publication No. 05-10026.)

OTHER HELP FROM SSI: Most people who get SSI can also get food stamps and Medicaid assistance. Medicaid, which is a different program from Medicare, helps pay doctor and hospital bills for people with low incomes. (For information about food stamps see Publication No. 05-10101.)

MEDICARE

Medicare is our country's basic health insurance program for people sixty-five or older and for many people with disabilities. You should not confuse Medicare and Medicaid. Medicaid is a health insurance program for people with low income and limited assets. It is usually run by state welfare or human service agencies. Some people qualify for one or the other, some qualify for both Medicare and Medicaid. (For information about Medicare see Publication No. 05-10043.)

Medicare has two parts:
- Hospital insurance (sometimes called "Part A"). This helps pay for inpatient hospital care and certain follow-up services.
- Medical insurance (sometimes called "Part B"). This helps pay for doctors' services, outpatient hospital care and other medical services.

ELIGIBILITY FOR HOSPITAL INSURANCE (PART A):
Most people get hospital insurance when they turn sixty-five. You qualify for it automatically if you are eligible for Social Security or Railroad Retirement benefits. You may qualify on a spouse's (including divorced spouse's) record. Others qualify because they are government employees not covered by Social Security who paid the Medicare part of the Social Security tax.

If you have been getting Social Security disability benefits for twenty-four months, you will qualify for hospital insurance.

People who have permanent kidney failure, who require maintenance dialysis or a kidney replacement, qualify for hospital insurance if they are insured or if they are the spouse or child of an insured worker.

Almost everybody qualifies for hospital insurance through one of the above methods. If you don't qualify and if you are sixty-five or older, you can buy hospital insurance just like you can buy other health insurance policies.

ELIGIBILITY FOR MEDICAL INSURANCE (PART B):
Almost anyone who is eligible for hospital insurance can sign up for medical insurance. Unlike Part A, which was paid for by your taxes while you worked and is free when you are eligible for it, Part B is an optional program that costs $36.60 per month. Almost everyone signs up for this part of Medicare.

ACQUIRING MEDICARE: If you are already getting Social Security benefits when you turn sixty-five, you will be automatically enrolled in Medicare (although you have the opportunity to turn down Part B). If you are disabled, you will be automatically enrolled in Medicare after you have been getting disability benefits for twenty-four months (and you can turn down Part B if you want). If you turn sixty-five but plan to keep working and do not plan to sign up for Social Security benefits at that time, you should call or visit a Social Security Office so they can help you decide if you should sign up for Medicare only.

There are many other rules associated with Medicare enrollment including penalties for not enrolling in Part B when you are first eligible. Please contact your Social Security Office for more details.

WHAT MEDICARE PAYS FOR: Medicare hospital insurance helps pay for:
- Inpatient hospital care.
- Skilled nursing facility care.
- Home health care.
- Hospice care.

Medicare medical insurance helps pay for:
- Doctors' services.
- Outpatient hospital services.
- Home health visits.
- Diagnostic X-ray, laboratory and other tests.
- Necessary ambulance services.
- Other medical services and supplies.

WHAT MEDICARE DOES NOT PAY FOR: Not all health services are covered by Medicare. Medicare does not pay for:
- Custodial care.
- Dentures and routine dental care.
- Eyeglasses, hearing aids and examinations to prescribe and fit them.
- Nursing home care (except skilled nursing care).
- Prescription drugs.
- Routine physical checkups and related tests.

HELP FOR LOW-INCOME MEDICARE BENEFICIA-RIES: If you get Medicare and have a low income and few resources, your state may pay your Medicare premiums and, in some cases, other out-of-pocket Medicare expenses such as deductibles and coinsurance. Only your state can decide if you qualify. To find out if you do, contact your state or local welfare office or Medicaid agency. (See Publication No. 05-10079.)

WHAT YOU NEED TO KNOW AFTER YOU SIGN UP FOR SOCIAL SECURITY

People who get Social Security should let the Social Security Office know when something happens that might affect their benefits. The following are some examples:
- If you move.
- If you get married or divorced.
- If your name changes.
- If your income or earnings change.
- If a child is born or adopted.
- If a beneficiary is imprisoned.
- If you leave the United States.
- If a beneficiary dies.

IF YOU DISAGREE WITH A DECISION SOCIAL SECURITY MAKES: When Social Security makes a decision that affects your eligibility for benefits or SSI benefits, they send you a letter that explains the decision. If you disagree with the decision, you have the right to appeal. If after reviewing your case the Social Security staff decides it was wrong, the decision will be changed.

There are three steps in the appeals process available within the Social Security system. Beyond these steps, you can take your case to a federal court. (See Publication No. 05-10041.)

You have the right to be represented by a qualified person of your choice when dealing with staff at your Social Security Office. (See Publication No. 05-10075.)

HOW YOUR EARNINGS AFFECT YOUR BENEFITS: There is a provision in the law that limits the amount of money you can earn and still collect all your Social Security benefits. This provision affects people under the age of seventy who collect Social Security retirement, dependents' or survivors' benefits. Earnings in or after the month you reach age seventy will not affect your Social

Security benefits. People who work and collect disability or SSI benefits have different earnings' requirements and should report all their income to the Social Security Office.

If you are under age sixty-five, you can earn up to $7,680 in 1993 and still collect all your Social Security benefits. However, for every $2 you earn over this limit, $1 will be withheld from your Social Security benefits.

If you are age sixty-five through sixty-nine, you can earn up to $10,560 in 1993 and still collect all your Social Security benefits. However, for every $3 you earn over this limit, $1 will be withheld from your Social Security benefits. This includes only the earnings you make from a job or your net profit if you are self-employed. This includes compensation such as bonuses, commissions and vacation pay. It does not include such items as pensions, annuities, investment income, interest, veterans or other government benefits. (See Publication No. 05-10069.)

YOUR BENEFITS MAY BE TAXABLE: Some people who get Social Security will have to pay taxes on their benefits. Generally, this provision affects people in the higher income tax brackets. If you file a federal tax return as an individual, you might have to pay taxes on your Social Security benefits if your combined income exceeds $25,000. "Combined income" means your and your spouse's adjusted gross income plus nontaxable interest plus one-half of your Social Security benefits. If you file a joint federal tax return, you might have to pay taxes on your Social Security benefits if your combined income exceeds $32,000. If you are married but file a separate federal tax return, you probably will pay taxes on part of your Social Security benefits.

Most people don't pay any taxes on their Social Security benefits. Of those who do, nobody pays taxes on more than one-half of his or her benefits. Some pay taxes on a smaller amount of their benefits according to a special formula contained in the law. (See IRS Publication 915 and Publication 554.)

HELP MANAGING YOUR BENEFITS: Sometimes Social Security or SSI recipients are not able to handle their own financial affairs. In these cases and after a careful investigation, a relative, a friend or another interested party is appointed to handle their Social Security matters. This person is a "representative payee." All Social Security or SSI benefits due are made payable in the representative payee's name on behalf of the beneficiary.

If you are a representative payee, your responsibilities are:
- You must use the Social Security or SSI benefits for the personal care and well-being of the beneficiary. Any excess funds must be saved on the beneficiary's behalf.
- You must keep Social Security informed of any events that might affect the beneficiary's eligibility for benefits. For example, you should tell Social Security when the beneficiary dies.

(See Publication No. 05-10076.) All Publications mentioned can be obtained free of charge at any Social Security Office or by calling (800) 772-1213.

MEDICAID

Medicaid pays for health care for certain needy residents of the United States. Medicaid is supported by federal and state taxes and may have a different name in your state as this program is state run. This section tells about who can get Medicaid, the services available to those determined eligible for full or restricted benefits, the choices for getting services, how to use the Medicaid card and stickers and your appeal rights if you feel you are treated unfairly or do not get what you are entitled to get by law.

You can get Medicaid benefits regardless of sex, race, religion, color, national origin, sexual orientation, marital status, age, disability or veteran status. Your local County Welfare Department manages the Medicaid program.

ELIGIBILITY FOR MEDICAID: Even if you are working, own a house, are married or not a U.S. citizen, you may be eligible for Medicaid. To get Medicaid, you must fall into one of the following Medicaid program categories:

- Public Assistance: If you are sixty-five years old or older, blind or disabled and getting Supplemental Security Income, you will get a full-benefits Medicaid card automatically. Your Social Security District Office can give you more information.

- If you are getting Aid to Families with Dependent Children (AFDC), you may also be entitled to get Medicaid benefits. If you are getting other kinds of public assistance, you may be entitled to all the services covered by Medicaid. Your county eligibility worker can give you more information.

- If you are not in one of these assistance groups, you still may be able to get Medicaid benefits in one of two categories called "Medically Needy" or "Medically Indigent." These programs are for people who cannot pay all their medical expenses. Even if you have other private health insurance coverage, you may still be eligible.

MEDICALLY NEEDY: You are Medically Needy if you are age sixty-five or older, blind, disabled, or you meet the family circumstances required for AFDC (you have minor children who are needy and do not have the support or care of one parent because of his/her absence, death, incapacity or unemployment). You can get a Medicaid card by paying or promising to pay medical expenses that equal your "share of cost" for the month.

MEDICALLY INDIGENT: You are Medically Indigent if you are a pregnant woman with no linkage to an AFDC program, a refugee in the country twelve months or less or a person age twenty-one to sixty-five in a skilled nursing facility or intermediate care facility. Persons under twenty-one years of age, including those in foster care whose needs are met by public funds; children who qualify for the state-only Aid for Adoption of Children; and certain other children not living with a parent or relative may also be included in this group.

SPECIAL PROGRAMS FOR PREGNANT WOMEN: If you are pregnant and cannot afford to pay for health care, Medicaid can help pay for medical expenses for you and your baby. Many times you can get Medicaid at no cost to you, even if you have income. Once you get Medicaid, increases in your family's income will not be counted during your pregnancy and for your baby's first year of life.

SPECIAL PROGRAMS FOR REFUGEES: If you are a refugee or entrant not qualified for the Medically Indigent or Medically Needy programs, ask your county eligibility worker for refugee entrant medical assistance.

CONFIDENTIAL MEDICAL SERVICES: If you are under twenty-one years of age, unmarried and living with your parents, you may get certain confidential medical services regardless of citizenship or immigration status. Under the Minor Consent program, you do not need parental consent to get a Medicaid card. Only your own income and property will be counted to determine eligibility. Medical services included under this special program are those which relate to family planning, pregnancy, drug and alcohol abuse, venereal diseases and other sexually transmitted diseases, sexual assault and mental health (which includes child or sexual abuse).

OTHER ASSISTANCE: You might qualify for medical assistance in one of the miscellaneous categories. Ask your county eligibility worker to help you. If you need specialized medical treatments such as dialysis treatment or parental hyperalimentation services, you may be eligible for services under one of the specialized treatment programs.

SPECIAL MEDICAID PAYMENT PROGRAMS: Some Medicaid programs such as the Buy-In Program and The Qualified Medicare Beneficiary Program will pay for Medicaid premiums, co-insurance and deductibles.

RESTRICTED MEDICAID BENEFITS: If you meet all other Medicaid eligibility requirements but are not a U.S. citizen and lawfully admitted permanent resident, or permanently residing in the United States under color of law, you cannot get full Medic-aid benefits. Instead, you may qualify for restricted Medicaid ben-efits which cover pregnancy-related care and/or emergency medical treatment only. If you apply for restricted Medicaid benefits, you do not have to answer any questions about your immigration status.

AMNESTY ALIENS: Congress passed a law in 1986 which granted amnesty to aliens who previously did not have the right to remain in the United States. If you are an amnesty alien and also blind, disabled, under age eighteen or age sixty-five or older, you may get full Medicaid benefits. If you are not blind, disabled, under age eighteen or age sixty-five or older, you may only get restricted Medicaid benefits during the first five years of your legalization.

MEDICAID FOR DISABLED PEOPLE: To get Medicaid as a disabled person, you must have severe physical and/or mental problems that will last at least twelve month and stop you from working during those twelve months, or cause you to die soon.

You must prove your disabling physical and/or mental problem(s) with medical records, tests and other medical findings. The medical problem must be the main reason why you do not work.

To get Medicaid for a disabled child, the child must have severe physical and/or mental problems(s) that are on a list of disabling childhood conditions or are so severe that he/she would not be able to do daily activities which a healthy child would be able to do.

MEDICAID PAYMENTS: You can get Medicaid regardless of how much money you earn or receive in other benefits. However, the more money you get, the more you will have to pay or promise to pay toward your medical bills before Medicaid will help pay your other medical bills.

PROPERTY/ASSETS ALLOWABLE FOR MEDICAID:

There are property/asset limits for the Medicaid program. If your property/assets are over the Medicaid property limit, you will not get Medicaid unless you lower them according to program rules. The county looks at how much you and your family have each month. If your property/assets are below the limit at any time during that month and you are otherwise eligible, you will get Medicaid. If you have more than the limit for a whole month, you will be discontinued. The home you live in, furnishings, personal items and one motor vehicle are not counted. A single person is allowed to keep $2,000 in property/assets, more if you are married and/or have a family. If a child has property/assets or if a stepparent wants Medicaid for a stepchild, other rules may apply.

APPLYING FOR MEDICAID: If you are pregnant or in immediate need of medical care, ask the eligibility worker who interviews you for "expedited service." The County Welfare Department will process your application as fast as possible. Pregnancy is considered an immediate medical need. Be sure to tell your eligibility worker right away when you apply if you have a medical appointment soon. The usual application procedure is:

- Get a Medicaid application from the County Welfare Department in your area.
- Fill out the form(s) as completely as you can.
- You should apply for Medicaid "retroactive benefits" if you had medical services in the three months before the month you apply for Medicaid and you think you will need help from Medicaid to pay the bills. If you were eligible for Medicaid during the three months before the month you apply, even if you have paid the bills, Medicaid may pay these bills. You can apply for "retroactive" payments at the same time you apply for Medicaid. If you don't ask

for retroactive Medicaid until after you start getting Medicaid, you have up to one year to ask for Medicaid to pay benefits retroactively.

- When you apply for Medicaid, your eligibility worker will explain your rights and responsibilities. You must give any changes in address, property, income, family composition, other circumstances and private health insurance coverage to your eligibility worker within ten days.

- When you turn in your application you will be asked to choose one of two ways of getting services under the Medicaid program. You may choose the regular Medicaid card and stickers or you may sign up for a Medicaid health care plan.

- It may take up to forty-five days for your Medicaid application to be processed. If you are applying for Medicaid based on disability, your application process may take ninety days. If you think you have an immediate medical need, tell your eligibility worker and your application may be processed faster. You can speed up the process by bringing in the necessary information and paperwork quickly.

- You will get a letter in the mail telling you that your Medicaid application is approved or denied. If approved with a "share of cost," you will get a share of cost form in the mail. If approved with no share of cost, you will get a Medicaid card in the mail. If you choose to sign up for a Medicaid health care plan, you will get a health care plan card or other notification to verify that you are signed up and entitled to use your health plan benefits.

- If you do not get an answer to your Medicaid application within a month after you apply, call your eligibility worker.

APPLYING FOR FULL MEDICAID BENEFITS: The following items or some combination of them are required when applying for full Medicaid benefits:
- Social Security card(s)

- Medicare card(s)
- Naturalization document(s)
- Alien registration card(s)
- Pregnancy verification
- Income verification:
  a. Employee pay stubs or a statement from your employer showing gross earnings and deductions.
  b. Award letter or checks showing amount of pension or benefits, including Social Security and Veterans Administration benefits.
  c. State Unemployment of Disability award letter.
  d. Student loan grant award letter(s) or loan grant papers.
  e. Statement from providers of other income (contributions, refunds, child support, etc.).
  f. Self-employment information: Last year's tax return or current ledgers and current inventory, including business equipment and supplies
  g. Care costs for child/incapacitated person(s).
- Property tax statements for all property.
- Vehicle registration(s) for automobiles, boats, campers and trailers.
- All checking and savings account statements and trust account documents.
- All stocks, bonds and mutual funds.
- All deeds of trust, mortgages, other promissory notes and contracts of sale.
- All life insurance policies, including cash surrender value.
- All annuity policies.
- All burial trusts/prepaid burial contracts/information on burial plots.
- Documentation regarding the current value of all trusts.
- Payment book(s) for possible available income (unemployment benefits, state disability benefits, etc.).
- All policies/cards for health insurance you currently have or which are available to you.
- Application(s) for possible available income.

- Court orders relating to income and property.
- Lease agreements.
- Life estate documents.
- Copies of patient trust account ledgers.
- Rent receipts, current utility bills, or housing statement.
- Copies of child support orders or divorce decree.
- Social Security disability denial or discontinuance notice.

SHARE OF COST FOR MEDICAID: Depending upon your monthly income, Medicaid may determine that you have to meet a share of your costs before Medicaid will pay for your own or your family's medical expenses for the month. Once you have met your share of cost for the month, you will get a Medicaid card you can use to pay for the rest of your medical expenses for the month. Medicaid cards are subject to certain limitations.

Whether you will have a share of cost for a month, and the size of your share of cost, depends on how much money or income you and your family get for the month. Medicaid allows you to keep a certain amount of your family's income for your living expenses. Medicaid may also allow you to keep additional amounts of your family's income. Any income for the month that is more than the amount you are allowed to keep becomes your share of cost for the month.

In some families, the income of one person cannot be used to decide if another person has a share of cost. For example, income of a child cannot be used to decide whether a brother or sister, parent, stepparent or caretaker relative has a share of cost. Income of a stepparent cannot be used to determine whether a stepchild has a share of cost.

If you don't have any medical expenses during the month for which you want a Medicaid card, you do not need to show that you met your share of cost for that month.

If you are a Medicaid beneficiary and you have a very high-cost medical condition that requires a physician's care, Medicaid may pay your private health insurance premiums if it is cost effective.

If you are hurt by another person or hurt at work, you may use your Medicaid card to get services. You must report the accident or injury to your eligibility worker so that the Medicaid program can be paid back by the responsible party.

Medicaid may bill the estate of a Medicaid beneficiary who has died only if:

- Medicaid paid for medical services after the beneficiary's sixty-fifth birthday, and
- The deceased Medicaid beneficiary had no surviving spouse or minor or totally disabled child(ren), and
- The Medicaid claim against the estate does not create a substantial hardship on the heirs of the deceased Medicaid beneficiary.

APPEAL: You will get a Notice of Action form in the mail from the County Welfare Department whenever your Medicaid eligibility changes. If you disagree with a decision about your right to get Medicaid benefits, you should talk to your county eligibility worker. If you are still dissatisfied, you may ask for a state hearing through the County Welfare Department. On the back of your notice you will find how you can request a state hearing and where to send your request. If you disagree with the denial of a health benefit, you can also ask for a state hearing.

You must ask for a state hearing within ninety days from the date on which you believe the wrong action took place. If you ask for a hearing before the effective date of the action that stopped or lowered your Medicaid benefits, you may continue to get the same Medicaid benefits until the hearing.

At the hearing, an administrative law judge will review the County Welfare Departments actions to see if someone made a mistake. You must either go to the hearing or give written notice for someone to go in your place. You may bring others to represent you or act as witnesses. You may ask questions at the hearing.

CHAPTER 4

EDUCATION

Title 1X of the United States Education Act Amendments generally requires equal opportunity for men and women in all aspects of education. These laws cover public schools—elementary schools, high schools, community colleges, state universities and the schools in the private university system.

Laws requiring equal educational opportunity also apply to all private schools and universities that receive money from the federal government. In the 1984 Corve City case, the U.S. Supreme Court ruled that Title 1X was only applicable to programs that directly received federal funding. However, in the 1987 Civil Rights restoration Act, Congress added provisions to Title 1X which specify that if an educational institution receives any federal funding, then all of its programs must provide equal educational opportunities.

Educational institutions that are exempt from laws requiring equal educational opportunity for women include schools that train individuals for military service or the merchant marines; private institutions with traditional and continuing single-sex admissions policies; and educational institutions controlled by religious organizations with tenets contrary to the provisions of equal opportunity for women.

YOUR RIGHTS

Women who attend a public school, or a private school that receives federal money, are entitled to equal opportunity with respect to school admissions, enrollment in classes, financial aid and participation in sports and clubs. The rights outlined in this chapter do not generally apply to students at schools that receive no federal money. They also do not apply to the institutions listed above as being exempt.

ADMISSIONS: Public schools and private schools that receive federal money may not discriminate against either sex in their admissions policies. This means that any private school or college that receives money from the federal government must be open to both men and women. Educational institutions receiving federal money cannot discriminate in their admissions policies on the basis of marital or parental status.

Educational institutions receiving federal money cannot discriminate or exclude a woman from admission on the basis of pregnancy, childbirth, termination of pregnancy or recovery therefrom.

Affirmative action admissions programs in universities and graduate schools are legal. Such programs may take into consideration factors such as race, economic and cultural disadvantages, but they cannot discriminate in favor of one race to the exclusion of another.

COURSE WORK: Classes at public schools, and at private schools that receive federal funds, must be open to both sexes. Classes in homemaking, auto mechanics, gardening and shop must be open to both male and female students. However, sex education classes may be restricted to one sex.

Counselors must not discourage or guide young women away from certain careers such as electronics, medicine, law and police work just because the counselors believe such jobs to be "unsuitable" for women. Counselors must provide all students, male and female, with available information on all careers. Tell your school counselor what is of interest to you, and ask for all the available information about those careers.

SCHOLARSHIPS: Scholarships and financial aid must be made available to all students on an equal basis. Specific scholarships may be distributed on the basis of sex, but overall distribution of scholarship funds must be made in a manner that gives both sexes equal opportunity to receive financial aid.

Specific scholarships for men or women may be legal. For example, a women's club scholarship for the top woman senior in a high school may be allowable. However, the total amount of scholarship money available must be enough to give both men and women an equal opportunity to apply for and receive scholarships.

A post-secondary educational institution may provide a scholarship or financial assistance to an individual upon the basis of personal appearance, poise and talent as an award in a pageant in which participation is limited to one sex.

SPORTS: Men and women/boys and girls must have an equal opportunity to participate in sports offered at schools.

Equal opportunity does not mean that men and women/boys and girls must share the same toilets, locker facilities or use the same showers. Men and women are entitled to the same privacy in these facilities that they have always had. However, male and female locker rooms must be of equal quality.

Physical education classes must be coeducational. However, classes involving contact sports may be segregated by gender.

Equal opportunity does not mean that all teams must be coed. Separate teams may be offered for males and females where separate teams are necessary to meet the needs and abilities of the students.

Students of both sexes must generally be allowed to try out for a team non-contact sport if the school does not sponsor a team for the excluded sex. This is true only if overall athletic opportunities for that sex have been limited in the past.

Equal opportunity does mean that schools must provide equitable equipment, supplies, scheduling of games and practice times, travel and meet allowances, access to locker rooms, coaching, opportunity to receive academic tutoring, provision of medical, housing, dining and training facilities and publicity for girls' and boys'/men's and women's teams.

Schools may spend money unequally on sports for each sex, if the quality of the programs for each sex is comparable.

All coaching positions must be open to candidates of both sexes. The best qualified candidate should be hired. So, for example, a school cannot require all of its boys' teams be coached by men and all of its girls' teams be coached by women.

HOUSING AT SCHOOL: Coeducational schools may provide separate living accommodations for each sex. Such accommodations may be separate, but each accommodation must contain equivalent facilities.

SOCIAL ORGANIZATIONS AND ACTIVITIES: Most school activities must be open to enrollment for any qualified and interested student regardless of his or her sex.

Private single-sex activities and father-son/mother-daughter activities may sometimes be permissible, as long as opportunities for "reasonably comparable" activities are offered to students of both sexes.

Recipients of federal funds may make requirements based on vocal range or quality. For example, a soprano-alto chorus may be effectively limited to only women.

Private single-sex social organizations such as sororities and fraternities may be permissible.

GRIEVANCES AND ENFORCEMENT

If you feel that a school or college has discriminated against you because you are a woman, or because of your marital status, or if you feel that a school or college has discriminated against your daughter or son, you may wish to contact the appropriate administrator of the school. School districts are required to have a Title 1X coordinator and an established grievance procedure.

CHAPTER 5

HOUSING

According to law, it is illegal to refuse to rent or sell a home to someone based on his or her race, color, religion, sex, sexual preference, marital status, national origin, ancestry, blindness, other physical disability or any other arbitrary category. When you seek to rent or buy an apartment, condominium or house, the owner or his or her agent cannot refuse to deal with you solely because you are a woman, divorced or separated, living with someone to whom you are not married or gay. Also, with respect to housing agreements, a single person with children is entitled to be treated the same as a married couple with children.

Furthermore, it is illegal for a financial institution to discriminate in mortgage lending on the basis of race, color, sex, marital status, religion, national origin and ancestry.

DISCRIMINATION IN HOUSING

The United States Congress has passed laws which prohibit discrimination in any aspect of leasing, selling or financing of residential accommodations. Discrimination based on any arbitrary classification is outlawed.

ILLEGAL PRACTICES: The following practices are illegal in the United States if they are done to discriminate on the basis of sex, race, marital status, or other arbitrary classification:

- Refusing to sell, rent or lease housing.
- Discriminating in terms, conditions, privileges, facilities or services in connection with such.
- Canceling or terminating a sale or rental agreement.
- Providing segregated or separate housing.

• Discriminating in terms, conditions or privileges relating to financial assistance for the purchase, organization or construction of housing.

• Retaliating against persons who have complained about discrimination to enforcement agencies.

• Making inquiries concerning the race, color, religion, sex, sexual orientation, national origin, ancestry or marital status of an applicant for housing.

• Printing or publishing any notice with respect to the sale or rental of a residence which indicates a preference, limitation or discrimination.

It is not, however, unlawful for a person to discriminate when renting a room to one person in his or her own home.

HOUSING DISCRIMINATION BASED ON YOUR MARITAL STATUS: You have a right to equal housing opportunities regardless of your marital status. The fact that you are single, married, divorced or separated may not be used as a basis to refuse to provide you with housing or to treat you unfairly or more harshly than other people.

The law against marital discrimination includes the right to equal housing opportunities for single parents. A person may not discriminate against you just because you have children and are separated, divorced, unmarried or living with someone. Single parents must be treated the same as married parents.

A person may ask about your marital status if such information is related to whether you are financially qualified to purchase, rent or lease a home. For example, if your income consists of alimony payments received from an ex-spouse, an owner or his or her agent may ask for information about your alimony to determine your financial ability to buy or rent housing. However, a person may not use this information to discriminate against you because you are divorced, separated, single, married or living with someone to whom you are not married.

HOUSING DISCRIMINATION AND CHILDREN: It is illegal to arbitrarily discriminate against children in rental housing. It is illegal for an owner or his or her agent to refuse to rent housing to you simply because you have children under a certain age. Condominium Owners Associations also may not discriminate against people who have children.

Specially created senior citizen housing is an exception. It is legal to prohibit the sale or rental of homes to families with children in senior citizen housing.

It is illegal under federal law for adult-only mobile home parks to discriminate against families with children.

Any person who intimidates or interferes with the efforts of persons to sell or rent housing because of their race, color, religion, sex, family status, handicap or national origin can be fined or imprisoned.

LEGAL RIGHTS AND REMEDIES

If you have a complaint about a landlord, landlady or homeowner who refuses to rent or sell to you and you think you are being discriminated against, you may seek legal help.

If you are considering legal action related to a housing discrimination claim, you may file a complaint with the Department of Fair Employment and Housing. You may seek a settlement, an administrative action leading to the possible award of compensatory and punitive damages or permission for the department to go to court. You may also want to contact a private attorney.

CHAPTER 6

HEALTH CARE

This chapter covers several areas of health care that affect all women to some extent. Topics discussed in this chapter include birth control, abortion, pregnancy, sexually transmitted diseases (including AIDS), breast cancer and assorted other health care issues of interest to women.

Many of these topics are the subject of differing views and are best discussed with spouses, partners, parents, doctors, social service agency personnel, clergy and other experts.

BIRTH CONTROL

There is a wide range of birth control devices, each with its own benefits and drawbacks. The choice of a birth control method is highly individual, and can only be made by you in consultation with your doctor and your sexual partner as to what will best suit your particular needs. Also, there are medical risks with many kinds of birth control, so it is best to discuss with your doctor your own health condition and history of diseases to learn the health risks to you if you use birth control devices. Some methods of birth control appear to cause serious side affects in women who have certain health conditions.

No artificial birth control device or drug is 100 percent effective in preventing pregnancy. Further, birth control devices and drugs are effective only when used as prescribed. Listed below are some of the most common forms of contraception.

THE BIRTH CONTROL PILL: There is actually more than one kind of birth control pill. "The Pill" refers to a drug containing some combination of the hormones estrogen and progesterone. These hormones generally stop a woman from ovulating. Doctors and drug manufacturers advise caution in the use of birth control pills by any woman who has had any of the following: uterine or breast cancer, varicose veins, phlebitis, heart problems, stroke, sickle-cell anemia, liver problems, migraine headaches, irregular menstrual periods or hypertension, or by a woman who is breast feeding, who is over forty years of age or whose mother used the drug diethylstilbestrol (DES) before the woman was born.

Other drugs, such as morning-after pills, are usually prescribed only in emergency situations because such pills generally contain DES and other drugs believed to have harmful side affects to users. Birth control pills do not protect against AIDS and other sexually transmitted diseases.

THE DIAPHRAGM: A diaphragm is a rubber shield inserted by a woman each time it is used and it is worn internally. It must fit properly to be effective therefore, a diaphragm must be obtained through a doctor or family planning clinic. The diaphragm is most effective if used along with a spermicidal cream or jelly. The diaphragm has not been found to have harmful side affects for most women users. A diaphragm does not protect against AIDS or other sexually transmitted diseases.

THE INTRAUTERINE DEVICE: An intrauterine device (IUD) is a device inserted into the uterus that prevents a fertilized egg from attaching itself to the uterus. The IUD can only be inserted or removed by a medical professional. Use of an IUD may increase your risk of getting pelvic inflammatory disease, or it may become dislodged and cause an infection or puncture the uterus. An IUD does not protect against AIDS or other sexually transmitted diseases.

THE CERVICAL CAP: A cervical cap is a small, round cap made out of rubber or plastic that fits over a woman's cervix. A cervical cap must be prescribed and fitted by a medical professional. It works best when used with spermicidal jelly or foam. A cervical cap does not protect against AIDS or other sexually transmitted diseases.

THE SPONGE: The contraceptive sponge is made of polyurethane, an artificial substance. The sponge covers the opening to the uterus, and absorbs and destroys sperm. You do not need a prescription for a contraceptive sponge and it can be purchased in many stores. It is less effective than the pill, diaphragm or IUD. The sponge does not protect against AIDS or other sexually transmitted diseases.

THE CONDOM: A condom is usually made out of thin, latex rubber. It covers the erect penis and prevents sperm from entering the vagina. Condoms can be purchased in many stores; and they work best when used with a spermicidal jelly or foam. Condoms, when used correctly, provide some protection against AIDS and other sexually transmitted diseases.

THE FEMALE CONDOM: The female condom is usually made out of thin, latex rubber. It is inserted into the vagina and is shaped at the opening to the uterus to hold it in place. The female condom can be purchased at many stores, but because it is a relatively new form of contraceptive device, its availability is still limited. The female condom, when used correctly, will provide some protection against AIDS and other sexually transmitted diseases.

STERILIZATION: Sterilization is a medical procedure that makes a person permanently unable to have children. Both men and women can be permanently sterilized.

A woman may be sterilized by surgery on her fallopian tubes. Other surgical methods of female sterilization, such as removal of the uterus or ovaries, are major operations which involve greater pain and health risks than surgery on the fallopian tubes. You should get a second medical opinion before having any surgery. You and your doctor should discuss the types of surgery which involve the least amount of risk to you.

WHERE TO GET BIRTH CONTROL: Prescription birth control devices can be obtained through your doctor, local planned parenthood office or county health, free or community clinic. Prescribed contraceptives include the birth control pill, the diaphragm, the intrauterine device (IUD) and the cervical cap. Sterilization procedures must be performed by a licensed physician.

Non-prescription birth control devices such as the condom, female condom, sponge and spermicidal foams and jellies can be purchased in many stores by men or women.

Many states allow minors to obtain non-prescription contraceptives with little or no age limit. Many school districts distribute condoms free to students and make them available for the taking.

Women under the age of eighteen do not need their parent's permission to purchase birth control devices. They may get counseling and birth control devices, free or for a small co-payment, from your local planned parenthood office, free or community clinic or county health center.

If you are a woman under eighteen years of age, you are required to have your parent's permission to be sterilized. However, you do not need your parents consent to be sterilized when you are under eighteen if you are:

- Married.
- On active duty in the United States Armed Forces.
- At least fifteen years old, live apart from your parents or guardians and are self-supporting; or have received a declaration of emancipation in the state in which you live.

You do not need your husband's permission in most states to use birth control devices or to be sterilized, nor does your husband need your permission to have a vasectomy (male sterilization).

No one has the right to perform a sterilization operation on you without your full knowledge and consent. Any time you prepare to undergo surgery or stay in the hospital (especially for childbirth or abortion), you should discuss with your doctor the decisions that he or she may have to make while you are being treated. Tell your doctor your wishes regarding sterilization. If you suspect that a sterilization operation has been performed on you without your knowledge or consent, you may wish to contract an attorney.

No health facility, clinic, county hospital or hospital formed by a hospital district, which permits sterilization operations for contraceptive purposes to be performed therein, may impose nonmedical requirements such as age, marital status or number of children before they will sterilize you. Private hospitals may refuse to perform sterilizations, as well as abortions, in their facilities.

If you have been on welfare or if you qualify for welfare assistance, you may be able to obtain birth control counseling and treatment through the state family planning services. Contract your local Department of Health Services for more information.

If you do not qualify for welfare assistance, you may still obtain birth control information and treatment for whatever you can afford to pay at family planning centers and clinics that operate on a sliding scale fee basis. Safe and adequate birth control is available to all women, regardless of financial condition.

ABORTION

If you are pregnant and want to terminate your pregnancy, you can do so by having an abortion. Abortion is currently legal in all fifty states; although some states have restrictions. If you have decided to have an abortion, you should protect your health by seeking medical help as soon as possible. The U.S. Supreme Court held that as a federal constitutional matter, certain restrictions on abortions are permitted. Even after this decision, abortion is legal unless it is reinterpreted by the Supreme Court or changed by the voters.

If you suspect you are pregnant and you think you might want to terminate your pregnancy, seek medical help immediately. If you decide to have an abortion, the abortion is safest when performed as early in the pregnancy as possible. There may be a time restriction on abortions in your state.

Abortions must be performed by a licensed physician. Free clinics, public health clinics, county hospitals, women's health centers, some private doctors and hospitals, and planned parenthood clinics will perform abortions. Call your city or county state Department of Health Services for more information.

In most states, if you are married, you do not need your husband's permission to have an abortion.

If you are under eighteen, you may be required to have the consent of at least one parent to have an abortion, or the permission of the juvenile court. You should contact your local planned parenthood office to find out the status of this law in your state.

Alternatives to abortion may be discussed with persons at your local hospital, free clinic, planned parenthood or doctor's office. Also, refer to the directory in the back of this book.

PREGNANCY

It is beyond the scope of this Handbook to discuss pregnancy. However, it is important for women to be aware of their rights in regard to pregnancy-related issues. Pregnancy can be both a rewarding and a long and difficult experience. For the health of the mother and child, it is important for a pregnant woman to have good medical care and good nutrition while pregnant. The following is a list of aid available to pregnant women.

THE PREGNANCY FREEDOM OF CHOICE ACT: The Pregnancy Freedom of Choice Act helps unmarried pregnant women under age twenty-one. If you are pregnant, under twenty-one years of age, unmarried, and if you intend to carry your pregnancy to full term, you can receive free counseling care as well as the service of a licensed maternity home. Your parents will not have to pay for any services that you get under the Pregnancy Freedom of Choice Act. For more information contact your local Department of Health Services or your local County Health Department.

HIGH RISK PREGNANCY: If you are experiencing a high risk pregnancy, you may be able to get help from the state toward specialized treatment. The programs that may be available to you include:

- Consultation and education about your particular high risk situation.
- A high risk infant follow-up program.

These programs are available to high risk pregnant women on a sliding scale fee system. This means that you will be charged only what you can afford to pay. If you would like more information about these programs, call your local office of the Department of Health Services.

INFERTILITY: In many states, group disability insurance policies must offer coverage for infertility treatment. You should check with your local Department of Health Services or the state Department of Insurance.

SUPPLEMENTAL FOOD PROGRAM FOR WOMEN, INFANTS AND CHILDREN: As explained in Chapter Two, good nutrition is very important during a baby's growth and development. You may be eligible for the special supplemental food program for women, infants and children (WIC) which provides nutritious food supplements and nutrition counseling to pregnant and nursing women, as well as infants and other children.

SEXUALLY TRANSMITTED DISEASES

Sexually transmitted diseases, particularly AIDS, should be guarded against. Sexually transmitted diseases can cause temporary discomfort, permanent damage or even disfigurement. AIDS, on the other hand, KILLS and can be very easily spread to spouses, partners, children and loved ones without either party knowing until it is too late. Your awareness of sexually transmitted diseases, their symptoms, methods of transmission, effects and cures should be taken very seriously.

ACQUIRED IMMUNE DEFICIENCY SYNDROME (AIDS): "WOMEN DO GET AIDS." In 1988 about eight percent of all people with AIDS were women. AIDS is a virus which attacks the body's immune system and makes it difficult to fight off other types of illnesses. This virus is usually fatal.

The following are ways that you can contract AIDS:
- By having sex with someone who is infected with AIDS, (through contact with that person's blood, semen, vaginal secretions, urine or feces).
- By sharing intravenous needles with someone who is infected with the virus.
- By receiving blood transfusions or blood products from someone infected with AIDS. (In 1985 blood banks adopted blood screening guidelines for AIDS so the chance of getting AIDS from a blood transfusion has been greatly reduced.)
- By using sperm from an infected donor for artificial insemination. Licensed sperm banks test seminal fluid to reduce the risk of AIDS infection from artificial insemination.
- By being a baby born to, or breast fed by, a woman infected with AIDS.

The following are ways you cannot contract AIDS:
- Through casual contact with someone infected with the AIDS virus. You can only be infected with AIDS through the exchange of bodily fluid—blood, semen, vaginal secretions, urine or feces—with someone who has the AIDS virus.
- By giving blood at a licensed blood bank. Licensed blood banks use thoroughly sanitary needles to take your blood. You are not at risk of getting AIDS when you give blood to a licensed blood bank.

Precautions to take against getting or spreading AIDS:
- Do not allow the blood, semen, vaginal secretions or urine of your sex partner to enter your body unless you know that he or she is not infected.
- Use condoms for vaginal, oral or anal sex. The AIDS virus cannot get through a properly used, unbroken condom. The receptive partner, the one whose anus is being pen-

etrated, is the one most at risk of contracting AIDS through anal sex.

- In addition to a condom, use a contraceptive foam, cream or jelly; they contain the spermicide Nonoxynol 9 which kills the virus on contact.
- Use rubber dams or other oral barriers for oral vaginal sex.
- Do not share intravenous needles, including tattoo needles with anyone.
- Do not have sex with an intravenous drug user who you know, or suspect, uses unsterilized needles.

AIDS AND PREGNANCY: If you are infected with the AIDS virus, you could give it to your child. If you have the AIDS virus, there is a fifty percent chance that you will give birth to a child who will be infected with the AIDS virus. A child can get AIDS from an infected mother during pregnancy, childbirth or breast feeding.

If you are infected and you want to have a child, it is important that you get regular medical help from a doctor who knows about AIDS. You may also want to get emotional support from a counselor or from group therapy. Ask your doctor for names and telephone numbers of local agencies or organizations that offer support and counseling to pregnant women who have AIDS. You can also refer to the directory at the back of this book for assistance

AIDS TESTING: If you have multiple sexual partners or suspect that your sexual partner may have other sexual partners, you should request an AIDS test from your doctor, free clinic, county hospital or women's health center. It is your right to ask that your sexual partner(s) also show proof of an AIDS test before having sexual relations with that partner. Remember, AIDS KILLS. You also may have contracted the AIDS virus through means other than sexual transmission, and AIDS testing can help identify the presence of the virus and stop it from being spread further.

If you are the victim of a violent crime in which bodily fluids are exchanged and if the crime could have resulted in the transmission of the AIDS virus, you may be able to ask the court to order the defendant who has been charged with the crime to undergo an AIDS antibody test. If you are the victim of such a crime, consult the district attorney who is handling your case about this provision. The results usually cannot be used in any criminal proceeding as evidence of either guilt or innocence.

Generally, it is illegal for someone to test you for the AIDS antibody without your knowledge and informed consent to such a test. In addition, it is generally illegal for your doctor to give the results of your AIDS antibody test to someone else without your written authorization unless that person is believed to be your spouse.

However, if you test positive for AIDS antibodies, a doctor may be able to inform someone reasonably thought to be your sexual partner, or someone reasonably believed to have shared a hypodermic needle with you, that they may have been exposed to AIDS without disclosing who might have exposed them to it.

With certain exceptions, before you are given a blood transfusion, all donated blood must be tested for AIDS antibodies.

Many cities, counties and states have passed local ordinances or laws and statutes, prohibiting discrimination against people with AIDS or HIV infection. Discrimination against people with AIDS or HIV infection in public accommodations and the provision of business services is usually illegal. Discrimination in employment against people with AIDS, where there is no likelihood of transmission of the virus, is usually illegal under most state laws.

OTHER SEXUALLY TRANSMITTED DISEASES: There are a wide variety of treatable sexually transmitted diseases (STDs, also know as venereal disease, or VD). STDs range from cervicitis to vaginitis. Most STDs can be treated by some sort of antibiotic. One of the most common forms of sexually transmitted diseases which affects women is chlamydia. Chlamydia, and other STDs, can cause sterility. If you suspect that you may have a sexually transmitted disease, the best thing to do is to go to your doctor, local health clinic or planned parenthood to have it diagnosed and treated. Use of a condom can help prevent the spread of most STDs.

BREAST CANCER

Breast cancer strikes about one out of every eleven women in the United States. It is the major cancer killer of women; its main target is women over thirty-five. Some seventy-five percent of all women with breast cancer are over fifty.

Breast cancer can be detected in a number of different ways. Some breast cancer is detected by breast self-examination or by a doctor's examination. Mammography, a low dose breast x-ray, can detect breast cancer much earlier than a physical examination.

There are a number of different methods of treating breast cancer. You and your doctor can decide what is best for you. The options include radiation therapy, drug therapy and assorted forms of surgery.

BREAST CANCER AND THE LAW: Under the law of all states, the codes of professional medical conduct require that your doctor advise you of all surgical and other alternative treatments for breast cancer. You have the right to choose surgical procedures less extreme than a radical mastectomy.

Most insurance companies are required to cover the cost of mammograms if they provide health service plan contracts, policies of disability insurance, self-insured employee welfare benefit plans or nonprofit hospital service contracts that provide coverage for mastectomy.

DES

According to the Planned Parenthood Federation of America, DES was given to some pregnant women between 1948 and 1960 to prevent miscarriages. DES was later discovered to be linked to genital abnormalities in children and to cancer in women who were given the drug during pregnancy.

If you were given drugs to prevent a miscarriage or if you are a child of a woman who was given drugs while she was pregnant with you, it is important that you see a doctor and undergo a series of medical examinations to detect and treat any abnormalities that re-sulted from DES.

DES may be currently prescribed as a "morning after" birth control pill. If you are in an emergency situation which requires you to use a "morning after" pill, you may wish to ask your doctor if he or she can prescribe a drug compound which does not contain DES.

PRESCRIPTION DRUGS

Some states allow pharmacists to substitute a generic drug for a name brand drug that has been prescribed for you. The substi-tuted drug must have the same active chemical ingredients, strength, quantity, dosage, and must be of the same generic type (as accepted by the U.S. Food and Drug Administration) since the same drug under one trade name may cost more than the drug sold under an-other name in the same generic form. Doctors often prescribe the better known and advertised trade name drugs. You may ask the pharmacist to substitute the generic type drug. A pharmacist may not substitute unless the drug product selected costs you less than the prescribed drug. A pharmacist may not substitute if the doctor indicated verbally or in writing that he or she does not want any substitution for a prescribed drug. When a substitution is made, the pharmacist must tell you that the substitution was made and place the name of the dispensed drug product on the label.

YOUR RIGHTS IF YOU ARE IN A MEDICAL EXPERIMENT

Before you may be asked to be a subject in a medical experi-ment, you must be given a copy of "THE EXPERIMENTAL SUB-JECTS BILL OF RIGHTS." This Bill of Rights must be in writing and in a language in which you are fluent. The list of rights must include the following:

- You have a right to be told of the nature and purpose of the experiment.
- You have a right to be given an explanation of the proce-dures to be followed in the medical experiment, and any drug or device to be used.

- You have a right to be given a description of any attendant discomforts and risks reasonably to be expected from the experiment.
- You have a right to be given an explanation of any benefit to you reasonably to be expected from the experiment if applicable.
- You have a right to be given a disclosure of any appropriate alternative procedures, drug or devices that might be advantageous to you, and their relative risks and benefits.
- You have a right to be informed of any avenues of medical treatment if any exist, available to you after the experiment, if complications should arise.
- You have a right to be given an opportunity to ask any questions concerning the experiment or the procedures involved.
- You have a right to be instructed that consent to participate in the medical experiment may be withdrawn at any time and that you may discontinue participation in the medical experiment without prejudice.
- You have a right to be given a copy of the signed and dated written consent form.
- You have a right to be given the opportunity to decide to consent or not to consent to a medical experiment without the intervention of any element of force, fraud, deceit, duress, collusion or undue influence on your decision.
- You have a right not to be subjected to any medical experiment unless you have been fully informed and voluntarily consented. If you have been subjected to a medical experiment without your full voluntary and informed consent, contact your local district attorney or a private attorney.

OPERATIONS MUST BE APPROVED

It is illegal for a doctor to perform an operation on you without your voluntary and informed consent. Before you are operated on, your doctor must describe the risks of the operation to you. You have a right to know about the medical care you are receiving. If there is something you do not understand or that you want your doctor to explain more fully, just ask. It is generally a good idea to get a second medical opinion before undergoing any form of major surgery. You always have the right to give or deny approval for any medical procedures, including surgery, for your minor children.

DURABLE POWER OF ATTORNEY FOR HEALTH CARE

Any person can authorize another person to make health care decisions for him or her. A document must be signed and witnessed by two adults personally know to you and acknowledged before a notary public. The person given your power of attorney to make health care decisions for you can consent to your doctor not giving treatment or stopping treatment necessary to keep you alive, although he or she cannot authorize anything illegal, contrary to your known desires or, where your desires are not know, anything clearly contrary to your best interest. Unless you indicate otherwise, the person can also authorize an autopsy, donate your body or parts of it for transplant or educational purposes, and direct the disposition of your remains. Without such a power of attorney, medical and other decisions may be made by your spouse or next of kin.

The power of attorney exists seven years from the date of execution of the written document creating it (or for a shorter time period if designated), unless at the end of the seven-year period the person granting the power of attorney lacks the ability to make health care decisions for himself or herself, in which case it will last until he or she can make those decisions.

Power of attorney should be considered by people who are living together but unmarried, particularly gay or lesbian people, to give the partners the same legal ability to make health care decisions as married people.

NATURAL DEATH ACT: The Natural Death Act recognizes the right of an adult to make a written directive to his or her doctor instructing the doctor to withhold or withdraw life-sustaining procedures in the event the person becomes incurably ill. Many states have variations on this act. Your doctor or a lawyer should be consulted before major surgery is performed. In addition, your intentions should be stated in writing or conveyed verbally to your spouse or next-of-kin.

RIGHT TO REFUSE MEDICAL TREATMENT: The courts have recognized that a competent adult patient with serious illness has the right, over the objection of his or her physicians and the hospital, to have life-support equipment disconnected, despite the fact that withdrawal of those devices will hasten his or her death, as long as he or she is advised of treatment options. There is no legal requirement that prior judicial approval is necessary. This right to refuse medical treatment may be exercised by the patient's conservator on his or her behalf, if he or she is incompetent to act for himself or herself even if the patient has not signed a power of attorney explicitly authorizing such action.

NURSING HOMES (COMMUNITY PROPERTY STATES)

If you, as a married person, enter a long-term care facility, such as a nursing home, only half of your community property, including income, is taken into account in determining your eligibility for Medicaid benefits to pay for the nursing home care. You will be required to spend your half of the nonexempt community property and all of your nonexempt separate property before being eligible for Medicaid benefits. You may transfer all of your interest in the home you own with your at-home spouse without affecting Medicaid eligibility.

HEALTH CARE RESPONSIBILITY

Relatives, other than spouses, are generally not held to be financially responsible for the cost of health care received by an adult.

CHAPTER 7

DOMESTIC RELATIONS

Husbands and wives and parents and children, have certain legally defined rights and responsibilities toward one another. This chapter discusses the legal rights of people within such relationships. Topics discussed include: marriage, cohabitation, divorce, surrogate parenting and responsibility for children, including adopted children and children of unmarried parents.

Most of the legal rights described in this chapter can be found either in family law or in the personal relations sections of your state civil code.

MARRIAGE

Marriage creates legal rights and duties between husband and wife. Marriage affects rights of support, property, taxes, inheritance and other matters discussed in this chapter. According to many states' laws, through marriage, husbands and wives contract toward each other obligations of mutual respect, fidelity and support.

REQUIREMENTS FOR MARRIAGE: There are a number of requirements that must be met before a woman and a man can legally be married. Usually, both parties to a marriage must be consenting adults eighteen or older. Many states allow women to marry as young as sixteen and a few as young as fourteen . However, if you do not meet the age requirement of your state, you may marry with the written consent of at least one of your parents or your guardian, and in some states a court order granting judicial permission for the union will suffice. The court may require those who are not of legal age to participate in premarital counseling.

A marriage license is usually required to marry. To obtain such a license, the parties in question must submit to blood tests for syphilis and, generally, rubella. In addition, in many states you must be offered a test for AIDS, but you are not required to have the test. If you do decide to have the test, you cannot be refused a marriage license if your test results indicate that you have been infected.

There are procedures for marriage without health certificates and with a confidential license for people who have been living together, but the confidential marriage license is only valid for ninety days from its issuance and only within the county where it was issued.

Only persons of the opposite sex may legally marry, and finally, a marriage must be solemnized by an authorized person. A legal marriage may be performed by a judge or a retired judge, a commissioner or retired commissioner of civil marriages, an assistant commissioner of a court of record or justice court in your state, by any judge or magistrate of the United States or by any priest, minister or rabbi of any religious denomination. The person conducting the ceremony must be at least eighteen years old.

You do not have to change your name when you get married. Once you are married, you may keep your birth (maiden) name, take your husband's name, or hyphenate your own birth name with your husband's name. You are not required to take your husband's last name upon marriage.

RIGHTS AND RESPONSIBILITIES

Upon marriage each spouse enters into an agreement to support the other and each spouse is committed to using whatever resources are available for this purpose. If there is inadequate community property to provide support for your spouse, you are expected to expend your own separate property to support your spouse.

COMMUNITY PROPERTY STATES: Some states have community property laws. If you were married in a community property state or lived there during your marriage, everything you or your spouse own is either "community" or "separate" property. Unless you and your husband agree otherwise, all property that is acquired by you and your spouse through either of your labor or skills during the marriage is community property. This includes property both in and out of your state of residence. Each spouse owns one-half of all community property. This is true even if only one spouse worked outside the home during the marriage and/or the property is held in the name of only one spouse. If you were married in a state that does not have community property laws and, while married you and your spouse purchased a home or other property in that state before moving to a community property state, the house will be treated as community property when you get a marriage dissolution in the community property state. This is true whether the property was bought with the earnings of either or both spouses during the marriage. This kind of property is called "quasi-community property."

During marriage, both husband and wife have an equal interest in all of their community property. Each spouse has the right to manage and control that property for the good of the family. This does not mean, however, that either you or your husband may sell or lease, for longer than one year, or give away real estate or personal property acquired during your marriage without written consent or the signature of the other spouse. "Real estate" includes a home, land, or rental property. "Personal property" includes furniture, clothing, cars, money and other personal goods. Each spouse owes a "duty of good faith" in dealing with the community property. This duty of good faith includes the obligation to make a full disclosure to the other spouse of the existence and extent of all community assets and debts. This obligation can be enforced through a court proceeding.

If you or your husband manage a business or an interest in a business which is substantially community property, the spouse who manages the business or interest has primary, not sole, control or management of the business. The managing spouse must give the other spouse notice of any major transactions. While the failure to give notice will not invalidate the transaction, the adversely-affected spouse may institute legal action to rectify any damage done to his or her interest in the business.

Some community property can be protected from your spouse's debts. Under "homestead laws," both husband and wife may declare a house and land as their homestead and thereby protect the house and land against claims of creditors. The law limits the amount of property that is protected by homestead rights. For information about declaring your property a homestead, contact the office of the county recorder in the county in which the property is located or contact an attorney.

Separate property includes all property that you or your spouse owned before you married. Separate property can also include certain gifts and any inheritance that one of you received either before or during marriage. Separate property can also include your earnings or your spouse's earnings, if you have entered into a premarital or marital property agreement in which the earnings are to be separate property and not community property.

Any earnings made after you and your spouse are separated are the separate property of the person who earned the money.

Community property laws are based on the Spanish legal system. There are eight community property states:

- Arizona
- California
- Idaho
- Louisiana
- Nevada
- New Mexico
- Texas
- Washington

COMMON-LAW STATES: Marriage in a state whose laws are based on the English common law system, is not to be confused with common-law marriages, which will be discussed later. Common law is an accumulated body of legal principles based on reason as applied by past court decisions. It emphasizes "precedent," something that has already been established by a court, as its guiding principle. The laws of the United States, (except Louisiana whose laws are based on Roman law or legal codes) are based on common law. There are forty-two common-law states. There is no book establishing common law; however, all courts are reluctant to overturn or depart from the common-law precedent. Each court's opinion of what the common law is may be different.

Under traditional English common-law marriages, when a woman married, she and her husband became "one," they became "husband." Everything became his, but he had the duty of caring for the family. His widow was entitled to the income from one-third of his lands for life and the right to live on the homestead. Such rights for women still exist in many states today.

While all states have passed laws specifically enabling a woman to hold property and most states permit her to convey the property without her husband's consent, title to personal property is often placed in the husband's name by tradition or for business reasons. Anything not specifically given to the wife from the husband's estate, remains his.

You should check the laws and statutes of your state in regard to your legal status rights as a wife in a common-law state.

JOINT TENANCY: Joint tenancy is another way for two or more people to own property together. Under joint tenancy each owner has an undivided joint ownership in the property with a "right of survivorship." When one owner dies, the entire property passes to the other owner. For example, if you own property in joint tenancy with your husband, you will not be able to leave any part of that property to your children or anyone else. Upon your death, your interest in the property would pass automatically to your husband.

The use of joint tenancy ownership may reduce the need for probate of an estate. However, it does not eliminate the obligation to pay inheritance and estate taxes. "Probate" refers to the required court proceedings following a property owner's death. Through probate, the decedent's property is given to the remaining family members or friends according to the will and to state laws. Probate can be costly and time consuming. If you have substantial assets, it is advisable that you contact a lawyer or tax accountant.

TENANCY IN COMMON: Tenancy in common is the third way that two or more people may own property together. Under tenancy in common each owner holds an equal interest as his or her separate property. If a married couple holds property as tenants in common, either spouse may sell or give away his or her interest in the property. Under both the community property and tenants in common methods of ownership, when one owner dies, his or her share of the property will pass to other persons according to the directions in his or her will or, if there is no will, to the deceased's descendants following the direction of state law.

A lawyer, banker or other financial advisor can best explain to you the advantages and problems of owning property in each of these ways.

ENFORCEABLE AGREEMENTS: There are three types of enforceable agreements within marriage—pre-marital agreements, agreements within marriage and agreements with other persons.

AGREEMENTS BEFORE MARRIAGE: Two people planning to marry may enter into an agreement before marriage (prenuptial or premarital agreement) concerning their future rights after marriage to property, earnings and other assets. So long as the prenuptial agreement does not promote dissolution of the future marriage, or vary the personal duties and obligations resulting from the marriage contract itself, it may be enforced in a court of law. Such an agreement should be consented to and signed by both parties, and may be recorded in the appropriate county offices.

AGREEMENTS BETWEEN HUSBAND AND WIFE: During marriage, a couple may also make an enforceable agreement covering rights to property and support. A written agreement is the easiest agreement to enforce, however, a written agreement is not required. Nonetheless, there must be an actual agreement, that is a meeting of the minds between husband and wife. This may be proven in court by the way the couple conducted themselves or by testimony from persons who were told about the agreement.

AGREEMENTS WITH OTHER PERSONS: Agreements made by either spouse with other persons during the marriage may be paid for out of the community property. Some types of agreements, such as sale or purchase of real property, may require the signature of both spouses. However, there are many kinds of agreements that either spouse can enter into without the signature or consent of the other spouse.

THE WIFE WHO EDUCATES HER HUSBAND: Divorce often occurs when the husband is ready to begin a professional career after the wife has spent years working to support him through school. Rarely are there any substantial assets to divide and the wife is not usually entitled to alimony. She has supported not only herself, but both of them. This situation has created many problems for the courts. It is easy to see that the husband has been the one to gain and the wife will not share his future success. Only a few states have addressed this problem and in those which have, there is, of course, a split.

Generally, in divorce law the longer the marriage, the greater the award to the wife. Payment for a spouse's education tends to work in reverse to this general principle. If the parties were married for twenty years after the wife helped the husband obtain his professional degree, courts would tend to say that she had reaped the benefits of his increased earning capacity by a higher standard of living during the marriage and that she is now receiving a fair share of property accumulated from those greater earnings. The equity increases, however, in the shorter marriage, where there has been no opportunity to accumulate assets and before the wife has had a chance to enjoy the higher standard of living which would have resulted from the professional education.

FINANCIAL AND LEGAL RIGHTS WITHIN MARRIAGE: When you are married you may file a "joint" tax return with your spouse, or a "married filing separate" tax return. State and federal tax laws are complicated. Various tax decisions will be of special importance to you because you are married. Tax issues of particular concern to married couples include joint and separate filing inheritance and estate tax planning, homestead rights and your possible liability for tax fraud committed by your spouse. You may wish to seek advice on these and other tax matters from your local tax office, the Internal Revenue Service, or from a tax specialist or private attorney.

When you are married, all parental authority over you ceases, even in you are under eighteen years of age.

In most civil proceedings brought by or against your spouse, you have a right not to testify. However, in some types of cases, such as certain criminal cases, juvenile court cases and commitment procedures, you may lawfully be asked to testify against your spouse. You may also be required to testify against your husband if he beats or rapes you.

In some states either spouse may sue the other for damages from personal injuries. If your claim is successful, any money or property your husband pays you must first be paid from his separate property, unless the injured spouse gives written consent to the use of community property for this purpose. After that fund is exhausted, he can use community property to satisfy the judgment. Whatever you receive as payment for personal injuries is considered your separate property.

COMMON-LAW MARRIAGE: A common-law marriage is defined as an agreement between parties who are legally free to contract a marriage to live together as man and wife. If established in a jurisdiction that recognizes common-law marriages as valid, the marriage is legal and binding on each party. There is no overall time frame for common-law marriages except as designated by state law.

Some states do not recognize common-law marriages; others either recognize them or have recognized them in the past. If you live in a state that currently does not recognize common-law marriages but did so in the past, you may have earned legal claim to property from the time the common-law marriage was recognized. You should seek legal advice to determine the status of your particular circumstances.

The following is a list of states which currently recognize common-law marriages:

- Alabama
- Colorado
- District of Columbia
- Georgia
- Idaho
- Iowa
- Kansas
- Montana
- Ohio
- Oklahoma
- Pennsylvania
- Rhode Island
- South Carolina
- Texas

If you are a common-law wife in a state allowing common-law marriages and you move to another state which does not recognize common-law marriages, you should contact an attorney to establish your rights in that state.

INHERITANCE—WILLS AND COMMUNITY PROPERTY

Your will is your legal instruction indicating who will receive your property after you die. Each spouse has the power to leave separate property and one-half of the community property to any person, according to his or her will. A will can be a formal document drawn up by an attorney and signed by witnesses. Equally valid in many states, is a "holographic will." This is simply a handwritten statement of how you want your property disposed of after your death. It must be dated (day-month-year), signed and written entirely in your own hand (no part of it may be typed). If you leave no will or an invalid written will, state law will determine who receives your property.

RIGHTS AS THE SPOUSE OF THE DECEASED: The surviving spouse is entitled to at least one-half of the community property on the death of the other spouse. The power of the deceased spouse to dispose of community property and quasi-community property to other persons by a will is limited to half of the property. The deceased spouse may, of course, specify in a will that all community and quasi-community property is to go to the surviving spouse. If the deceased left no will, the surviving spouse will receive all of the community and quasi-community property.

In most cases, it may be necessary to go to court to confirm title to community property left by a deceased spouse. These court procedures are simplified in cases involving only community property left to the surviving spouse, and do not require probate administration of that portion of the estate.

If a husband or wife died leaving separate property but no will, the separate property usually will be distributed under law between the surviving spouse and deceased's children. If there are no surviving offspring, then the property will be distributed among the surviving spouse and lineal descendants or parents and siblings of the deceased.

You can get support payments while your husband's estate is being settled. If you were dependent on your husband for all or part of your support, the court has discretion to grant you, your children and any other dependents, an allowance while the estate is being settled. Also, you should contact your local Social Security office to determine your eligibility for survivors' benefits.

DISSOLUTION OF MARRIAGE—GROUNDS FOR DIVORCE

In the United States, each state has its own laws on marriage and divorce. The legal reasons for which divorce may be granted are called "grounds." They vary widely among the states, but generally are fault-related, that is, blame is placed on one of the partners. Nearly every state recognizes adultery as grounds for divorce at the request of the innocent partner, and most also recognize cruelty, desertion and habitual drunkenness. Other common grounds are nonsupport, conviction of crime, impotence, insanity and mental cruelty. Some states permit a marriage to be dissolved when both partners claim incompatibility of temperament or irreconcilable differences.

Some states provide for no-fault divorce (called "dissolution of marriage"). This means that to dissolve your marriage, it is not necessary to prove that you or your husband have done something wrong; it is only necessary to convince the court that you and your husband have irreconcilable differences. Generally, in the case of a no-fault divorce, the only time specific acts of wrongdoing in the marriage are pertinent is when the acts are relevant to the award of custody of the children.

Irreconcilable differences mean that there has been a serious breakdown in the marriage and that there are convincing reasons why the marriage should not continue. As a practical matter, if you and your husband agree that there are irreconcilable differences and that your marriage cannot continue, the court will usually grant the dissolution without question. However, if it appears to the court that you and your husband may be back together again, the court may delay the dissolution proceedings to allow you time to reconcile.

Insanity of one of the spouses as a ground for dissolution must be proved by medical evidence from a medical doctor or psychiatrist. Divorce on the grounds of insanity does not relieve the spouse from an obligation to support the insane spouse in most cases. If the mentally ill spouse does not have a guardian, the court will appoint one for him or her.

A person applying for divorce must reside in the state where the application is made. A specific period of residence is required, most commonly, one year. To attract divorce business, some states have adopted more lenient divorce laws regarding grounds and residence requirements. For example, in Nevada you can file for divorce without having any grounds for divorce and without being a resident of Nevada.

WHAT YOU SHOULD KNOW BEFORE FILING FOR A DIVORCE: First and foremost you should know where everything is. Know the location and account numbers of identifying features of all your assets: bank accounts, safe deposit boxes, wills, insurance papers, storage units, stocks, bonds, mutual funds, credit unions, IRA accounts, 401K accounts and the like. If your husband is a small businessman and has a partnership or corporation or is a professional and has a professional corporation, find out about partnership agreements, buy-sell agreements, ownership of property and anything else of importance affecting the value of his business interest.

Anything not currently held in a joint account, such as bank accounts, property, insurance policies and the like, need to be made joint survivorship legal ownership. You should also get a copy of your husband's will. This document can be very helpful in proving your husband's intent to take care of your needs after his death, and therefore can have an effect on the divorce settlement. This document may also inform you of assets you did not know existed.

You should "Money" check your health insurance policy as divorce services may be covered at either fifty or eighty percent. "Money" check means that your medical insurance policy may have provisions for coverage, up to eighty percent, for the costs of your divorce if the divorce is required because of health reasons (usually mental health reasons).

Know your debts. Write down what debts exist and what notes or mortgages you personally have signed.

You should start setting aside money to hold you over until the court awards you living expenses during the divorce process. This money should be under your own name in your own account, not a joint account. Courts can always decree temporary support to you and the children, but two or three months may go by before you get a hearing before the judge.

A dissolution proceeding is begun when either spouse files a petition for dissolution with the state Superior Court and serves a copy of the petition and summons on the other spouse. The court cannot grant a divorce decree by default but must require proof of the alleged grounds either before the court or by affidavit. This process can be handled by you with very little guidance. Free legal aid is available for women. You can contact a "legal clinic" and if you qualify, will be given the documents to fill out and told about the necessary fees and procedures you will have to follow to file for a divorce. If you think property received by gift or inheritance during the marriage; his or your separate property; property acquired before the marriage; separate earnings; rights to future income; workmen's compensation settlements; cash value of life insurance policies; retirement contributions and/or benefits; personal injury awards or claims; disability income payments; business interests; goodwill of a business; or increase in value of separate property are problems which may affect your divorce, then you should get a lawyer or confer with a paralegal before filing for divorce. This is also true in community property states. Remember, you may not get another chance to present your claims so be as complete as possible with all financial and property information.

The amount of time you will spend in court depends on a number of factors. Hearings for uncontested dissolutions do not take very long. However, a hearing for a contested dissolution may take hours, days or even longer. Your dissolution can become final only when you have been issued a final judgement. The final judgment is a paper that must be signed by the judge and entered into the official court records by the county clerk before your marriage can be dissolved. You cannot legally remarry until you receive your final judgment.

There is sometimes a simpler way to obtain a dissolution. It is called a "summary dissolution." A summary dissolution makes it unnecessary to appear in court, to serve a summons or to file an interlocutory judgment. This procedure may be used in most states only if all of the following circumstances exist:

- You meet the residence requirements.
- Irreconcilable differences have caused the irremediable breakdown of the marriage and the marriage should be dissolved.
- There are no children of the parties (either born or adopted before or during the marriage) and the wife is not pregnant.

- The duration of the marriage does not exceed the state requirement for this procedure at the time of the filing of the dissolution petition.
- There are no real property interests at the time of the dissolution. A residential lease, occupied by either party, that will terminate within a year of filing the divorce petition, and that does not include an option to purchase the residence. This is not considered a real property interest for this purpose.
- Community debts do not exceed a certain amount (usually these do not include automobile debts).
- The total fair market value of the community property is less than a certain amount, adjusted for inflation.
- Neither spouse has more than a certain amount of separate property (usually does not include debts and automobiles).
- The parties have made a property settlement agreement and have executed (signed) the documents necessary to carry out the agreement.
- Both parties give up any rights to spousal support.
- Both parties, upon entry of final judgment, give up any rights to appeal or to move for a new trial unless fraud, duress, accident, or mistake is involved.
- Both parties have read the summary dissolution brochure provided by the court.
- Both parties want the court to dissolve their marriage.

If all of the above requirements are met, the parties may file a joint petition (signed by both husband and wife) for summary dissolution. If you would like the court to issue an order that restores your birth name, you may so state on the joint petition for summary dissolution. After a designated waiting period of such a joint petition, the court may issue a final judgment dissolving the marriage.

Either party has the right to revoke the petition for summary dissolution at any time before a request for final judgment is made. You will remain married until one of you files for and obtains a final judgment of dissolution. If either of you revokes the petition for summary dissolution before the final judgment is entered, the dissolution process will be terminated until a new petition is filed.

CONTESTED DIVORCE: In some states, the wife must specifically ask for each and every item she wants. The complaint also requests that child support, alimony, attorneys' fees and all payments for debts and services be paid by the husband. The husband usually has thirty days to answer the complaint either admitting or denying each of the wife's statements. He may file with his answer a cross-complaint. If no cross-complaint is filed, either party, or the court, may then set a date for trial. If a cross-compliant is filed, the wife must answer the husband's charges within thirty days. When her answer is filed, a court date may be set.

If a wife has no means of support, all states require a husband to provide support for his wife and children before the final divorce. The United States Supreme Court has held that, under the Constitution, a wife may not be denied access to the courts because of her lack of funds. Therefore, all states have provisions for ordering suit money and temporary support during the divorce proceedings. Your local court may not grant you living money, attorneys' fees or anything else, but it has the power to do so. Any money received as alimony, even under a temporary order or under a signed agreement is taxable to the wife. However, money paid during separation, without a court order or not in writing between the parties, is taxable to the one who earned it.

If you ask for and are granted exclusive use of the marital home, also request that your husband be required to continue to make the mortgage payments. Ask that he pay the property taxes and house insurance, and be prevented from termination of the telephone and utilities service and any insurance without application to the court to do so. You may also request that the court restrain him from intercepting any telephone conversations on the home telephone.

If you go to trial you must have a lawyer. If there is a court decision you do not like, you have three choices:

- You can accept the decision and live with it;
- You can request a rehearing from the trial judge; or
- You can appeal the decision.

If you are still unhappy with the rehearing decision, you can appeal. You only have a certain number of days to request a rehearing or an appeal so you must react quickly if you are not satisfied with the decision. The number of days may vary according to individual state rules of procedure. Most time limits set by law are absolute; however, time limits set by an agreement and approved by a judge can be changed if approved by a judge.

Be sure that all property you want is requested before the divorce, not after. If you do not present your claim to property where legal title is only in the name of the other spouse, it the property of the other spouse. Community property states are the exception.

A decision in a divorce court must, by statute, be equitable within the trial court's discretion. You are guaranteed equity, which is defined as "fairness and justice." "Discretion" is defined as "acting according to one's own judgment." Ultimately the decision you receive will reflect what your local judge thinks is fair and just. Even on appeal these words are frequently heard; "recognize that there are inequities which may result from the failure to compensate the spouse."

DIVISION OF ASSETS (COMMUNITY PROPERTY STATES): Community property laws mean that generally one-half of all community property belongs to you and one-half belongs to your husband when you divorce. Community property generally includes both of your earnings while you were married and living together. When you get a dissolution, you and your spouse each keep the separate property you own. Separate property includes real estate, money, furniture or any other belongings that you or your spouse owned before marriage. It also includes certain gifts and inheritances you received before or during marriage. Separate property held in joint tenancy may be subject to the court's jurisdiction.

It is possible for separate property to become community property. For example if you put separate property money that you inherited in a savings account with mostly community property money, it may become community property. It is also possible, if the married couple lives in and pays taxes or a mortgage on a house that was the separate property of one of the spouses, that house may become community property. There are many other complications in deciding whether your possessions are separate or community property. A lawyer may help you resolve these questions and arrive at a proper settlement.

Community property money used for the education, training or repayment of education-related loans of one spouse may have to be repaid to the community property before a settlement of community property. If the contributions substantially enhance the earnings capacity of that spouse and if there is no express written agreement of the parties to the contrary, any debts incurred before or during the marriage for the education or training of one spouse will be considered to be that spouse's separate property debt upon dissolution of the marriage in most cases.

Except for education or training-related debts, debts that either you or your spouse acquired during marriage are community property debts. This includes credit card bills, even if the card is in your name only. Community property possessions and community property debts are divided equally, unless you and your spouse agree to an unequal division.

Money you owed before getting married or debt you acquired after separating from your spouse is your separate property debt. Each of you is responsible for paying your separate property debts.

You and your husband may own more community property than you realize. Many married couples own a home, furniture, appliances and a car as community property. You and your spouse also may have cash in checking and savings accounts, stocks and bonds, pension and profit-sharing plans, life insurance policies, tax refunds or tax debt, a vacation home, rental property or a business, all of which can be community property. Even though each spouse usually keeps his or her clothing and jewelry, these belongings may be community property too.

A lawyer can help you make sure that all belongings are properly listed as either community or separate property. Your lawyer can explain any rights you may have to your spouse's pension or profit-sharing plan or retirement benefits and whether you are entitled to a share of your spouse's Social Security payments. Your lawyer also can tell you whether money you or your spouse receives from a personal injury lawsuit or worker's compensation claim qualifies as community or separate property.

A minority of progressive states have held in the past that the wife divorcing a military husband was entitled, by her equal service to the family, to share in the retirement benefits earned by the husband.

You and your spouse can decide how to divide your community property belongings. You can divide them any way you like, even if the division is not equal, as long as you both agree to the division of property. This can be a complicated process, and each of you may want a lawyer's advice. You also might want to save money by having one lawyer, especially if you and your spouse agree on matters of property division, support and custody.

If you and your spouse cannot agree, the court must decide how to divide your possessions. If a judge believes that the value of your community property is more than a certain amount, or if he or she believes the parties are unable to agree on a division of the property, you may have to submit to arbitration. If you do not like the arbitrator's decision, you can then go to court. If your community property adds up to more than a certain amount, a judge will decide for you. Unless there are unusual circumstances, your belongings will be divided evenly. However, the court might not split the ownership of each of your belongings between you and your spouse; instead, it might give each of you things of equal value. For example, if your spouse gets the furniture and appliances, you might get the family car or something else of equal value.

Often, your house is the most valuable community property you and your spouse own. All your other possessions added together may not equal the value of your house. If you and your spouse cannot agree on what to do with your house, the court will make the decision. The court might say the house should be sold and the profits divided equally between you and your spouse. If you have young children, the court might say that the spouse who has custody can live in the house and that the house should be sold when the youngest child is eighteen years old. This is know as a "deferred sale of home order." Ask your lawyer to explain other ways that you and your spouse or the court might settle the problem of what to do with your home.

Once the court approves the property settlement that you and your spouse agree to, you cannot make changes unless both spouses agree in writing and the court approves.

PROTECT YOURSELF: You can protect your share of the community property while your divorce is pending. If you are afraid that your husband will endanger the community property or your separate property while your dissolution is pending, you may ask the court to issue a protective order. You can ask the court to order your husband not to take any action which changes your property interest without first obtaining your consent. For example, the order may forbid your husband (or you) from selling, concealing or mortgaging any real or personal property. The order may also forbid your husband (or you) from making any expenditures that are not for the usual necessity of everyday living.

MILITARY RETIREMENT: You may be eligible to share in the military retirement benefits your husband earned. A minority of progressive states have held in the past that the wife divorcing a military husband was entitled, by her equal service to the family, to share in the retirement benefits the husband earned. Under federal law, a court may treat federal pension rights, including military pension rights, either as the sole property of the pension member, or in accordance with state law that treats pension rights, as either community property or an asset of both the pension member and the spouse. State courts cannot treat as property divisible upon divorce military retirement pay that has been waived by a veteran in order to receive veterans' disability benefits.

SPOUSAL SUPPORT/ALIMONY: "Spousal support" is the legal name for alimony. Spousal support is money paid by one spouse to another after they have divorced or legally separated. Spousal support can be awarded at any time, for any length of time to either the husband or the wife. You and your spouse can decide if one of you should receive spousal support.

If you and your spouse cannot agree about alimony, the court will decide. The court will decide whether spousal support should be paid, who will pay it, how much will be paid and how long it will last, but the court does not order spousal support in all cases.

You can receive spousal support while you are waiting for your divorce to become final. Once you file a petition to dissolve your marriage, your most urgent need may be for financial support for you and your children, especially if you are not working for pay and have relied entirely on your husband's earnings for income. If your husband has a job and you do not work for pay, the court will usually order your husband to pay temporary support. The amount you receive will be based on your needs, your children's needs and your husband's earnings.

Often the length of time you were married will help the court decide whether you or your spouse can receive spousal support and for how long. If you have been married twenty-five years and have never worked outside the home, the court might decide that your chances of finding a job are limited. Then, you might receive spousal support for life or until you remarry.

Suppose one spouse is young and has never worked outside the home? The court might say this spouse should receive spousal support until he or she either is self-supporting or receives training for a job. If both you and your spouse have jobs outside the home, the court might say neither of you is entitled to spousal support.

There are many issues that help the court decide about spousal support. For example, the court will consider both spouse's situations in terms of separate and community property, debts, health issues and standard of living. It also will consider any special needs each of you has, such as whether one of you has custody of minor children, the amount of money you and your spouse can be expected to earn, and the length of time it will take an unemployed spouse to train for and find a job. You also may be required to submit copies of your state and federal income tax returns to your spouse's counsel during the course of the litigation over spousal and/or child support.

The court may award spousal support after the divorce has been finalized. Perhaps neither of you needs spousal support when your marriage is dissolved, but needs can change. One spouse might have a long and expensive illness, or the business of one spouse might fail. Anticipating such problems, your lawyer may advise you to ask the court to "keep the door open" for a certain period of time. Then, you will be able to ask the court for spousal support in case your needs change during that period. As long as one of you is entitled to spousal support, you or your spouse may go back to court and ask the judge to increase or lower the amount whenever there is good reason.

Federal and state income taxes must be paid on any spousal support payments received. The spouse who makes the support payments can deduct the amount paid on his or her taxes.

You can lose most of your financial support from your ex-spouse if you have been living with someone else and therefore need less money. The court may reduce your support until there is a change in your economic circumstances and you need support again.

Unless otherwise agreed upon in writing, spousal support will cease upon the death of either party or upon the remarriage of the spouse who had been receiving the support.

CHILD CUSTODY

Subject to court approval, you and your spouse can decide with whom the children will live. There are two possible types of custody by parents—joint custody or sole custody. No matter which parent the children live with, each parent ordinarily continues to have a responsibility to his or her children.

SOLE CUSTODY: Sole custody means that one parent will be responsible for raising the children. The parent who does not have sole custody usually has "reasonable visitation" rights, unless the visitation would be detrimental to the best interests of the children. In other words, the parent who does not have sole custody can see the children at certain times and places that both parents agree upon. If the parents cannot agree, the court will set up a schedule. Reasonable visitation rights may also be granted to any other persons having an interest in the welfare of the child.

JOINT CUSTODY: Joint custody means that both parents are involved in making decisions about the children, such as where the children will go to school and where they will live. Joint physical custody means that both parents have significant periods of physical custody, and joint legal custody means that parents share the responsibility for significant decisions relating to the children's health, education and welfare. For example, the children might spend six months a year with each parent, or the children might spend more time with one parent than with the other.

COURT-APPOINTED CUSTODY: If you and you spouse cannot agree on custody, the court will make the decision. The court does not automatically give custody of your children to their mother. Instead, the court must decide which parent will serve the best interests of the children.

The court may decide not to give custody to either parent, but to a third party without the consent of the parents. However the court can only award custody to a third person if it finds that the award of custody to either parent would be detrimental to the children and that the award of custody to a third party is required to serve the best interests of the children.

The court will deal with the issue of child support and custody as quickly as possible. If you and your husband go to court and if the only contested issue is child custody, the court will speed up the process by giving you an early court date. If there are issues besides child custody, the court will separate the child custody issue and hear it immediately.

Most states have a court mediation proceeding to help resolve custody and visitation disputes. Unfortunately, many couples end up in courtroom battles over child custody and visitation rights. You must go to a mediator before your regular hearing if there is a dispute concerning custody or visitation rights with your children. The counselors will try to help you and your spouse settle your differences and make a recommendation to the court on a way to handle custody and visitation. Some states and counties offer other services that can help you and your spouse get back together, adjust to the dissolution or settle disputes over other issues besides custody and visitation.

The custody agreements you originally agreed to may be changed. If you later decide the custody arrangements you agreed to are not in the best interests of your children, you may, with or without an attorney, apply to the Superior Court in your county to mediate any child custody or visitation arrangements previously made in the Superior Court. Modifications of these previous arrangements may be made through the mediator in certain counties without formal court hearings. The agreements reached by the parties may be formalized by the judge of the Superior Court. If this mediation fails, you still have the right to petition the court for formal court hearings.

If you believe your husband will not appear at the child custody hearings with your children, you can get help from the district attorney. If your children are in your husband's possession and their whereabouts are unknown to you, you may ask the district attorney to locate your husband and compel him to appear at the custody proceeding with your children. Your husband may do the same if you have possession of the children and he has reason to believe you will not appear.

If your husband kidnaps your children, you are entitled to get help from the district attorney. If you have been awarded sole custody of your children and your husband takes the children from you in violation of the custody orders, you may ask the district attorney to take all actions necessary to locate your children and enforce the custody order. Child abduction is punishable by a jail, prison term and a fine or both.

CHILD SUPPORT

You and your spouse can work out a child support plan, but the court must approve the amount to be paid. If you cannot agree, the court will decide whether you should receive child support payments and how much they should be. If your husband has child custody, you could be ordered to pay child support to him. Among other things, the court will consider the income and earning ability of both you and your spouse and the ages and needs of your children. It will also consider whether you or your spouse are supporting other people, such as children from a previous marriage. The court will also consider the medical insurance of everyone involved.

Usually, child support payments are made until your children complete the twelfth grade or attain the age of eighteen, whichever occurs first. However, if you have a child under eighteen who gets married or becomes "emancipated" or self-supporting, the child support payments can be stopped.

Usually, at any time subsequent to one year after the entry of a previous order for the award of child support, either spouse may ask the court to change the amount of child support payments.

Unlike spousal support, the child support money you receive is not taxable. If one spouse pays more than half the cost of supporting a child, he or she usually can claim the child as a tax exemption. The two of you can agree who gets the tax exemption.

In many states if you receive public assistance and child support, your spouse must make the child support payments to you through the District Attorney's Office. This office is also responsible for making sure your spouse obeys the court's child support orders. If you receive public assistance, the court may also order your spouse to pay any alimony through the courts.

YOUR HUSBAND DOESN'T PAY HIS SUPPORT: You may get a court order to force your husband to pay the child support he has been ordered to pay. You may ask a judge to charge your spouse with "contempt of court" for disobeying a court order. The penalty for contempt may be a fine or jail or both and could be applied for each missed payment. Or he can be charged with a "misdemeanor." This is a criminal offense with penalties of up to one year in jail in most states. You may also ask the court to order your spousal or child support payments deducted from your spouse's paycheck, his unemployment compensation payments, his tax refunds or his lottery winnings and sent directly to you.

It could also save you a lot of trouble if you ask the court to order him to make payments directly to the clerk's office (if this is allowed in your state) and this way the court already has the record and the proof and you may be able to file by yourself without a lawyer for unpaid support payments. You must file against him each time he fails to pay for child support unless you go through the clerk. In some states, support will be paid directly to you through the clerk's office, and if the spouse doesn't send in his payments to them, the state will file a contempt proceeding.

Some states will, in appropriate circumstances, forgive or retroactively modify past due payments. If your ex-husband has been destitute for a year through no fault of his own, a state that will retroactively modify past due payments may reduce his liability under the original decree back to the time his hard luck began. States that will not retroactively modify past due payments, take the view that the payments are overdue and that he should have requested the court to change his payments when his bad luck began.

Under extraordinary circumstances when a parent is in arrears for child support payments and spousal support payments and has acted in bad faith, the court can order the parent to deposit assets to secure future payments with the district attorney, other county officer or other trustee designated by the court. These assets may be sold to pay the arrearage.

You may obtain a court order that your spouse be required to provide health insurance coverage for supported children and yourself if that insurance is available at no cost or at a nominal cost to the parent/husband. The court may also order a health insurance coverage assignment by the employer.

Congress passed the Family Support Act of 1988 and this law should be phased in from 1989 through 1994. Provisions require automatic withholding of child support payments from wages of all employees in most new child support orders after January 1, 1994, unless the parents have agreed otherwise in writing or where there is good cause for not withholding. Starting in 1991, states will be required to use specific guidelines for setting child support awards and beginning in 1994, will have to review and adjust the awards every three years for families on welfare or who have requested review.

PHYSICAL PROTECTION DURING THE DIVORCE PROCESS

If your husband has assaulted or threatened you and you fear that he will do so again, you may ask the court to issue a protective order, ordering your husband to stay away from your home, while your dissolution is in progress. If the court feels it is necessary, it may forbid your husband from contacting, molesting, attacking, striking, threatening, sexually assaulting, battering or disturbing the peace for you or those in your custody. If your husband knowingly violates the court orders, he is subject to criminal prosecution.

LEGAL SEPARATION

For some people, religious, economic or other reasons make a divorce undesirable. If you do not want a divorce, but you and your spouse are living apart and have no hopes of getting back together, you and your spouse may get a legal separation. Grounds for a legal separation are the same as those for a divorce. There usually is no residency requirement for a legal separation.

When you make a request for a legal separation, a property settlement and arrangements for spousal support, child support and child custody must also be made.

Property laws apply to legal separations just as they do to divorces. When you receive a legal separation, you are entitled to a determination by the court of all assets as in a divorce.

Usually if one spouse asks for a legal separation and the other spouse asks for a divorce, the court will proceed with the divorce.

If you and your husband are separated without a legal order and have no intention or hope of getting back together, your earnings after separation are your own, and your husband's earnings are his own. Such earnings are not entitled to a determination by the court and are not community property unless the spouses are merely living apart on a temporary basis.

A legal separation does not end your marriage. You cannot remarry unless you get a divorce.

VOIDABLE MARRIAGES

The legal term for an annulment is a "nullity." If you get a nullity, the court will say that legally your marriage never existed. The grounds on which a marriage is voidable are strict and most people do not qualify. Possible circumstances under which you may obtain a nullity include: if you were married at too young an age and without proper consent; if you were forced into marriage; if either party is of unsound mind or physically incapable of entering into the marriage state; if you wrongfully believed your first spouse to be dead; or if you married a non-U.S. citizen and later learned that he married you only to become a U.S. citizen. A lawyer can best counsel you on whether you meet the qualifications to receive an annulment. You may legally remarry at any time after the court grants you a nullity.

Marriages that are declared void are treated as if they never existed. Usually, after a marriage is declared void, it is legally as if the couple was never married.

If either or both spouses in a marriage that has been declared void believed in good faith that their marriage was valid, the spouse must be treated as a putative spouse. In such a case, what would have been considered dividable assets or community property in a marriage becomes quasi-marital property and is divided as the court sees fit or in the case of a community property state, divided equally.

Some marriages are void from the beginning. The grounds upon which a marriage is void are incest and bigamy/polygamy, with certain exceptions. A judicial proceeding must be filed to declare a void marriage a nullity.

BIGAMY

Bigamy is being married to two people at the same time. Bigamy is illegal and if you or your spouse are married to another person at the same time, your marriage is generally illegal and considered void. There are possible criminal penalties for committing bigamy. In most states, if your spouse is absent for more than five years and you believed him or her dead, then marrying again is not considered bigamy.

INCEST

Incest is defined as marriage for sexual intercourse between parents and children, any ancestor and descendent, brother and sister including half brother and sister, uncles and nieces, or aunts and nephews. Such marriages are void from the beginning. Incest is a criminal offense and is punishable by imprisonment.

Solemnizing incestuous marriages is forbidden. Doing so willfully and knowingly can lead to a fine or imprisonment. In addition, incest is cause for a voidable marriage.

LIVING TOGETHER WITHOUT MARRIAGE

Most states do not recognize cohabitation as a legal contract between two people, as they do marriage. However, the military recognizes some legal rights for cohabitants. Yet you do have some rights with respect to the person you are living with, particularly if you have some sort of written or verbal agreement. Also, if you have children by a man to whom you are not married, your children and their biological father have a legally protected relationship.

RIGHTS AND RESPONSIBILITIES: In all but thirteen states and the District of Columbia, you may not contract a common-law marriage (a common-law marriage is a marriage where two people live together with the intention of being married, but do not participate in the ceremony—see Common-Law Marriages). However, if you have contracted a common-law marriage in a state that recognizes such marriages to be valid, most states will recognize your common-law marriage as valid.

If you believed in good faith that you were legally married but your marriage is void or voidable, the court can declare you to be a putative spouse. If your marriage breaks up, you will then be treated by the courts as if you had been legally married with all the same rights and responsibilities as a married person seeking a divorce.

You may lose some or all of your spousal support (alimony) from a previous marriage if you have been living with a man and therefore need less money. Your alimony may be reduced by the court until there is a change in your economic circumstances and you need more money again.

Your husband must continue to pay the same child support, even if you are living with a man who contributes to the care and support of the children in your custody. If you are living with a man, he may adopt your children, but the children's father must usually consent to the adoption. If the man with whom you are living adopts the children, the court may reduce or discontinue your ex-husband's child support obligations.

If you have been living with someone without being married, you may have some rights if you separate. In the Marvin vs Marvin case the court upheld the enforceability of a verbal or written contract between two people living together. The California court held that where a man and woman live together and they make an agreement that one person will provide household services (excluding sexual services) with the reasonable expectation of being paid for those services, the person who performed those services has a legal right to be compensated at the agreed amount or at reasonable value for those services. The court ruled that when an unmarried couple separates, the court has the power to divide the property according to the couple's reasonable expectations during cohabitation. A presumption that the unmarried couple intended to deal fairly with each other will be applied by the court. However, intentions, expectations and agreements of two people are very difficult to prove if they are not stated in some form of written agreement.

If the person with whom you have been living dies without leaving a will, you will not inherit any of his or her possessions. His or her property will pass to his or her surviving family members. You might be able to claim a portion of the estate if you had an expressed agreement to pool your earnings and belongings. However, this is difficult to prove if your agreement was not in writing. For the protection of both parties, you and your partner should each prepare a will to insure that your intentions are carried out.

CHILDREN OF AN UNMARRIED COUPLE: Many states still categorizes children as "legitimate" or "illegitimate." The law usually says that the parent and child relationship extends equally to every child and to every parent, regardless of the marital status of the parents. Establishing a parent-child relationship is important for such things as inheritance, child support obligations, custody of children and adoption. Everything in this section applies to any man who is the father of your children, whether you ever lived with the man or not.

If you have a child with a man to whom you are not married, the father has the same obligations to the child as he would if he were married to you (the mother of the child). And the child has the following legal rights:

- A child born out of marriage has the same inheritance rights as a child born in marriage in most states.
- A child born out of marriage has the same rights to receive payments through his or her parent's Social Security, union and insurance benefits as a child born in marriage.
- A child born out of marriage may sue a third party for wrongful death of a parent.
- A child taken into the home of another and openly held out to be his or her child may have rights vis-à-vis that person.

A man is presumed to be the father of a child if any of the following conditions exist:

- The man and the child's natural mother attempted to legally marry each other before the child was born but for some reason the marriage is or could be declared invalid. If a child is born during the attempted marriage or 300 days after its end or 300 days after the end of cohabitation, the man is presumed to be the father.
- The man and the child's natural mother are or have been married to each other and the child is born during the marriage or within 300 days after the marriage ends. (The marriage could have ended by death, annulment, declaration in invalidity, divorce or a separation declared by the court.)

The following applies to you if your marriage ends while you are pregnant:
- The man and natural mother have married but the marriage could later be held invalid for some reason and the man is named as the father on the child's birth certificate with his consent; or the man is ordered by the court to support the child or voluntarily promises to do so.
- The man receives the child into his own home and openly holds out the child as his own natural child.
- The child was born and resides in a country with which the United States engages in an orderly departure program or successor program and the man acknowledges that he is the child's father in a declaration under penalty of perjury.

A presumption means that the court will hold the man to be the father of the child if any of the above circumstances exist, unless he can provide clear and convincing evidence that he is not the father.

You may get child support from the father of your child even if you were never married to him. If you want to establish that a man is the father of your child, you may bring an action in court. If the court decides that a man is the father of your child, the court may order him to pay for part of the child's support. The court can also order the father to help pay for part of the expenses you incurred during your pregnancy. The district attorney may also bring an action to establish paternity if he/she feels it appropriate to do so, as may a man presumed to be the child's father, the child or any interested party.

Unmarried parents may petition the court to receive assistance in developing custody and visitation plans. You do not need an attorney to receive such assistance in most states.

The Family Support Act of 1988 requires states by 1991 to substantially increase the number of cases in which paternity is established. By 1990 or later, the act will also require the tracking of Social Security numbers of both parents for every child born and by 1991 genetic testing, largely paid by federal funds, in all contested paternity cases. New state laws have been passed to implement this act.

Even if you were never married, the father of your child can request that the court give him custody or visitation. Refusal to allow a parent to exercise custody rights is a criminal violation in all states.

PARENTAL RESPONSIBILITY

According to state laws, the natural or adoptive parents of a child have equal responsibility to "support and educate their child in the manner suitable to the child's circumstances, taking into consideration the respective earnings or earning capacities of the parents." This may be enforced more easily when a child's biological parents are married and living together. However, regardless of the relationship between a child's parents, each parent has a responsibility to support his or her child. The sections on divorce and unmarried couples dealt with child custody and child support in those cases. This section will give you an overview of parent-child rights and responsibilities, and then will discuss alternative methods of becoming parents, particularly adoption, artificial insemination and surrogate motherhood.

RIGHTS AND RESPONSIBILITIES: While a child is a minor and unmarried, his or her parents are generally legally responsible to provide for that minor's support and education.

You may be held responsible for your child's actions. If a child willfully defaces or destroys property of another, causes injury to another or causes the death of another, a parent or guardian having custody or control of the child may be held responsible, along with the child, for the willful act. The parent may be held responsible for a fine for each willful act of the child, and the parent may be held responsible for medical expenses, dental expenses, in addition to any other liability imposed by law. A parent or guardian having custody or control may also be liable for court costs and attorney's fees.

There are a number of ways your child can cease to be your legal responsibility:

- The court can appoint a new guardian for the child. The court does not need your consent if it finds that you are an unfit parent.
- If a child is at least of a certain age, lives separate or apart from his parents or legal guardian with their consent or acquiescence, is managing his or her own financial affairs and is not deriving his or her income from criminal activity, the court can declare him or her an emancipated minor. If the court does so, the child becomes responsible for his or her own well-being.
- Once your child marries, he or she is no longer considered a minor, even if he or she is younger than eighteen and even if the marriage is dissolved.
- Anyone under eighteen who is on active duty in the military is considered an emancipated minor.

ADOPTION: Under most state laws the rights and responsibilities of adopted children and their parents are the same as those of natural children and their parents. After adoption, the biological parents of an adopted child are generally relieved of all parental duties and responsibilities toward the child. However, there are a number of issues unique to adoption situations.

REQUIREMENTS FOR ADOPTION: The person adopting a child (anyone under the age of eighteen) must be at least older than the child. Most states have established a certain number of years that the adoptive parents age must meet. However, if the adoption is by a stepparent, sister, brother, aunt, uncle or cousin of the child, and if married, the spouse thereof, the court may approve an adoption without an age difference, if it is in the best interest of the parties and in the public interest.

In most states, any adult person may adopt any younger adult who is not his or her spouse. In some states, you do not need to be married to adopt a younger adult.

Consent of both biological parents to an adoption is necessary unless:

- The parent(s) has willfully failed to support or communicate with the child for over a year when able to do so (the absent parent must be served with notice to appear in court).
- The court has deprived the parents of custody and control of the child.
- The parent(s) has deserted the child without provisions for identifying the child.
- The parent(s) has relinquished the child for adoption.

A person who is a minor may relinquish a child for adoption. Once consent is given for an adoption, it may not be withdrawn except with court approval.

Your spouse may not adopt a child without your consent unless you are legally separated.

DISCOVERING THE IDENTITY OF YOUR NATURAL PARENT OR CHILD

The birth parent may, at the time of adoption, or later, authorize the State Department of Social Services to provide the person who has been adopted with the name and address of their birth parent when the person reaches the age of twenty-one. This is true in most states if that person requests it, or earlier in the event of a medical necessity or other extraordinary circumstances.

Most states allow an adult adoptee, his or her natural parents and his or her adopted parents, to sign a waiver of his or her rights with respect to the confidentiality of the adoption record. If this is done, the Department of Social Services or any licensed adoption agency may arrange a contact.

It is possible in most circumstances, upon request, for the Department of Social Services or any licensed adoption agency to release to the adoptee, if eighteen or over; to the adoptive parents on the adoptee's behalf if he or she is under eighteen; or to the birth parents letters, photographs or other items of personal property. Identifying names and addresses will be deleted from such documents in most cases.

It is also possible for an adopted person to file a request for contact with natural siblings, with a waiver of confidentiality to grant siblings contact rights. The adopted person must be at least twenty-one for such a request to be made in most cases. If his or her siblings are also twenty-one or older and have filed such requests and waivers, contact can be arranged.

In some states, adoption records are sealed and may not be released to the birth parents or the adopted child. There are organizations which may be able to help you locate a birth parent or a child given up for adoption. See "Adoption" in the directory at the end of this book.

It is illegal for anyone to pay a parent for the placement for adoption, the consent to an adoption or for the cooperation in the completion of an adoption. However, it is not illegal to pay maternity-connected medical, hospital and living expenses during and immediately after pregnancy. Such payment cannot be contingent upon placement of a child for adoption, consent to the adoption or cooperation in the completion of the adoption. However, it is against the law for a parent to obtain these financial benefits with the intent not to complete the adoption or consent to the adoption.

You may be able to receive some financial assistance from the state and federal government if you choose to adopt a "hard to place child."

If the biological parents and their child ever lived together, the child may still have some rights of inheritance to the biological parents' property and their relatives' property.

Laws concerning adoption are very complicated and no two cases are exactly alike, making it very important for you to contact an adoption agency, adoption lawyer or the appropriate state agency to fully understand the legal implications of your particular situation.

ALTERNATIVE METHODS OF BECOMING PARENTS

Infertility in both men and women has opened up alternative methods of child bearing other than by both biological parents. Because the legal ramifications involved are beyond the scope of this text, only subjects with defined legal guidelines are discussed. Even though legal guidelines have been established, it is critical that you consult with a lawyer practiced in these issues in order to protect all parties concerned.

ARTIFICIAL INSEMINATION: Artificial insemination involves the fertilization of a woman's egg using sperm from a donor. In some cases, the donor is chosen by the recipient. In other cases, an unknown donor is used. Artificial insemination is one way for couples who cannot otherwise conceive to have children. It is also a way that single women can conceive.

The husband of a woman who has been artificially inseminated by the semen of another man is usually treated under the law as if he were the natural father of the child. In order for this to be true, the artificial insemination must have been done with the consent of the husband and under the supervision of a licensed physician. A MAN WHO DONATES SPERM IN AN INFORMAL INSEMINATION ARRANGEMENT MAY POSSIBLY ESTABLISH THAT HE IS THE CHILD'S FATHER AND MAY BE ABLE TO ACQUIRE VISITATION PRIVILEGES. He may also become liable for support.

SURROGATE PARENTING: A surrogate mother is usually paid a set fee by a couple pursuant to a surrogate contract to be artificially inseminated with the husband's sperm. Customarily, the contract is between the prospective biological father and the surrogate mother with an intermediary fertility center, organization or other party serving as a broker between the two parties. The contract provides that, after the delivery, the surrogate mother must give up her parental right to the child with the biological father receiving full custody rights. The husband of the surrogate mother also surrenders any claim to the child. Both the surrogate and her husband agree not to develop a parental relationship with the child. Paternity of the inseminating father is confirmed through genetic testing. The wife of the biological father is not a party to the contract. She adopts her husband's child upon the surrogate mother's relinquishment of her parental rights to the child.

Surrogate parenting agreements also may involve medical and psychological testing and screening of both the surrogate and inseminating father, a review of the medical records of the surrogate mother's other children and continued medical monitoring during the pregnancy. Contracts specifically may prohibit the surrogate mother from drinking alcohol, taking drugs or smoking, and may require that amniocentesis be performed. Contracts also may specify when the child is to be aborted and stipulate that the inseminating father and adoptive mother will take custody in the case of birth defects or multiple births.

Fees and expenses are delineated and the money is placed in escrow. Compensation of the surrogate mother in the event of a miscarriage and future attempts to impregnate the surrogate are also addressed. Most contracts provide for reimbursement for the surrogate's attorney fees and may include anonymity provisions. Some contracts include the surrogate's acknowledgment of the adopting couple's emotional investment in the arrangement in an effort to provide the latter with legal recourse for intentional infliction of emotional distress should the surrogate mother renege on the agreement.

Surrogate parenting contracts may be considered unenforceable (Baby M, NJ 1987) and many states have yet to rule on the legality of surrogate parenting. A lawyer must be involved in establishing the legality of surrogate parenting in your state and assisting in the contracting of surrogate parenting.

CHAPTER 8

RIGHTS OF WOMEN, VETERANS, SPOUSES AND DEPENDENTS

Women veterans are eligible for the same benefits as male veterans. Public law 98-160 directs that appropriate care be provided in a timely fashion to any eligible veteran for any gender-specific disability in addition to benefits available to men.

Women are eligible if they were active members of the following services:

- Air Force, Marine Corps, Coast Guard or Commissioned Officers' Corps of the U.S. Public Health Service.
- Served in the Women's Army Auxiliary Corps (WAAC) in World War II, 1942-43.
- Flew as a Women's Air Force Service Pilot (WASP) in World War II, or served as a telephone operator, clerk, dietitian or reconstruction aide with the Army in Europe during World War II.

MEDICAL BENEFITS

Any injury or illness incurred while in the service, and which has been ruled "service connected," gives you a category "A" medical service.

Former spouses of both active duty and retired personnel who were married at least twenty years, including fifteen years during the member's active duty service, are eligible for full military medical coverage if their divorce is final on April 1, 1985. These spouses are not eligible for exchange or commissary privileges.

Former spouses of active duty and retired personnel who were married at least twenty-nine years, including fifteen years during the member's active duty service and will be divorced after April 1, 1985, will be eligible for two years of military medical care. After two years of coverage, former spouses would have the option of buying low cost medical insurance provided by the U.S. Department of Defense. Former spouses having their own health insurance are not eligible for medical benefits. However, if they later lose civilian health insurance, they become eligible for the military coverage. All medical privileges terminate if the former spouse remarries.

OTHER BENEFITS

Guaranteed home loans are available. Educational benefits are also available, however, they depend on the type of program which was in force during your time in the service.

Former spouses of both active duty and retired personnel who were married at least twenty years during the member's active duty service may also receive exchange and commissary privileges. All exchange and commissary privileges terminate if the former spouse remarries.

SPOUSE OF VETERANS

A "spouse" under military definition is: A person of the opposite sex whose marital relationship to the veteran is valid under laws of the place where the parties resided at the time of marriage or the law of the place where the parties resided when the rights to benefits accrued.

COMMON-LAW MARRIAGE: The Veterans Administration (VA) recognizes common-law marriage. Common-law marriage is defined as "an agreement between parties who are legally free to contract a marriage to live together as man and wife." If established in a jurisdiction that recognizes common-law marriages as valid, the marriage is legal and binding on each party. There is no recognized time frame for common-law marriages for purposes of establishing a military recognized common-law marriage. Instead the VA follows the time limits established by the jurisdiction where the common-law marriage was recognized. Many states do not currently recognize common-law marriages. Some do and many have in the past (during which period a spouse may establish that eligibility was earned).

A person who is the spouse or child of a veteran is eligible for a number of benefits. Survivors of deceased veterans, spouses of living veterans and the children of either deceased or living veterans between eighteen and twenty-six years old, when the veteran's death or permanent disability was the result of service, are eligible for the survivors' and dependents' education program. Other programs available include pensions, death compensation, non-service connected death pension and dependency and indemnity compensation (DIC).

DISSOLUTION OF MARRIAGE: The VA has its requirements as to the dissolution of a marriage. There are three of these: divorce, annulment and the death of a spouse. Proof of death must be provided by one of the following methods:

- A copy of the public record of the state or community where the death occurred.
- A certified copy of the coroner's report of death or a verdict of a coroner's jury from the state or community where death occurred.
- A death certificate or clinical summary or other report showing the facility and date of death signed by a medical officer when death occurred in a hospital or institution under the control of the U.S. government.
- An official report of death of a member of the uniformed services from the Secretary of the Department concerned when the death occurred while the deceased was on the retired list, in an inactive duty status or in the active service.

In the absence of evidence to the contrary, a finding of fact of death by another federal agency will be accepted. When death is attributable to common disaster, evidence must be secured to show as definitely as possible that the disappearance and death were attributable to the catastrophe.

Military divorces that were final before June 26, 1981, cannot be reconsidered for military pensions, but divorces after that date may be reconsidered for a share of the pension awarded to the former spouse.

States that would divide military retirement pay, would divide it only if the military person had already reached the twenty-year mark and others would divide the pension regardless of whether the husband had reached the twentieth year. The wife's share would be paid if and when the service member retired and began receiving benefits.

It is important that you contact a lawyer on this subject as the laws vary from state to state. There are also a variety of different retirement plans of which you will need to be aware as to their legal effects on the Internal Revenue Service, courts, congress, legislatures, insurance companies and employers.

MISSING IN SERVICE: An official determination of death may be made in the case of a member of the armed forces missing in action at any time that the secretary of the service concerned determines that the facts so warrant. Otherwise, the general rule is that an armed force's member in "missing in action" status for twelve months will be presumed dead.

PRESUMPTION OF DEATH: For benefit purposes, state laws concerning presumption of death do not apply. A finding of presumption of death requires evidence establishing the continued and unexplained absence of any individual from home and family for seven or more years. If, after a diligent search, no evidence of existence after the date of disappearance can be found, the date of death will be established as the date of expiration of the seven-year period.

SURVIVING SPOUSES: A surviving spouse is a person who was the lawful spouse of a veteran at the time of the veteran's death; who lived with the veteran continuously from the date of marriage to the date of death, except when there was a separation which was due to the misconduct of or procured by the veteran without the fault of the spouse, and who has not remarried.

FORMERLY REMARRIED SURVIVING SPOUSE: A "formerly remarried surviving spouse" under military definitions is: A surviving spouse who has remarried and whose remarriage has been dissolved by death, divorce or annulment. These spouses may be restored to their former status.

INFERENCE OF REMARRIAGE: An "inference of remarriage" under military definition is: A surviving spouse who has not married but, since the death of the veteran and after September 19, 1962, lived with another person and held themselves out openly to the public to be the spouse of such other person. He/she may be ruled to have been remarried. A spouse formerly barred because of inference of remarriage may be restored as the spouse of the veteran if he/she ceases such relationship.

REMARRIAGE: Remarriage does not bar benefits to the surviving spouse of a veteran if the remarriage is void or has been annulled by a court of competent jurisdiction. For a void marriage, a certified statement from the claimant setting forth the circumstances that rendered the marriage void and other supporting evidence may be required. A certified copy or certified abstract of the decree of annulment is required to establish annulment.

DEPENDENTS OF VETERANS: The way the VA determines whether or not a dependent child of a veteran is eligible for benefits is just as complicated as everything else it does. The term "child of a veteran" means:

- An unmarried person who is a legitimate child.
- One legally adopted before eighteen years of age.
- A stepchild who acquired that status before the age of eighteen and who is a member of the veteran's household at the time of the veteran's death.
- An illegitimate child who is under the age of eighteen.

- One who before becoming eighteen becomes permanently incapable of self-support.
- One who is between the ages of eighteen and twenty-three pursuing a course of instruction at an approved educational institute.

The following are the types of children that the VA recognizes and the proof it requires for each:

- Legitimate Child: You must show that the birth is legitimate under state law by presenting a birth certificate or other acceptable evidence, or show that the mother was legally married to the veteran.

- Illegitimate Child: Proof that a father relationship exists when acknowledgment in writing has been signed by him; evidence identifying him as the child's father has been ordered by judicial decree; or secondary evidence supporting the relationship exists. The following serve as proof: public record of birth, church record of baptism, statements of persons, information from service departments or records of public agencies acknowledging the veteran to be the father.

- Adopted Child: The term means either a child who has a final decree of adoption, or an unrescinded interlocutory (an immediate but not final) decree of adoption while remaining in the custody of the adopted parent (or parents) during the interlocutory period. A child under eighteen who was a member of the veteran's household at the time of the veteran's death and was adopted by the veteran's spouse within two years of the date of death is also considered a child for benefit purposes.

- Stepchild: Evidence for a stepchild consists of proof of birth, evidence of the marriage of the veteran to the natural parent of the child, and evidence that the child was a member of the veteran's household at the date of the veteran's death.

- Child Adopted out of Family: A child adopted out of the family of the veteran either prior or subsequent to the veteran's death is nevertheless the veteran's child.

- Formerly Married Child: A child who was married and whose marriage is dissolved by death or divorce may be restored to the former status as a child of the veteran as long as his former entitlement exists.

CHAPTER 9

CHILD CARE

In the United States in 1940, 8.6 percent of all mothers with children under eighteen years of age were working outside the home. As the number of families with two working parents and the number of single parent households has grown since that time to well over ten million households, the need for quality child care increases.

This chapter describes basic, publicly subsidized, indirectly subsidized and private child care options available to parents. Also, there is at least one child care resource and referral agency in every county in each state. For help finding child care that will meet your needs, look in the telephone book for the number of the agency nearest you.

PUBLICLY SUBSIDIZED DAY CARE

Each state agency involved with the responsibility for publicly subsidized child care programs receives the bulk of its money from the state involved and services vary according to the state involved. However, national and local governments also provide funds for some forms of child care, and they have a say in how the child care money is spent.

In general, families whose annual income is below eighty-four percent of the state's median income are eligible for subsidized care. Those whose incomes are more than fifty-nine percent of the median must pay fees on a sliding scale in most states. Eligibility for care is discontinued when a family's income reaches 100 percent of the state's median income.

To qualify for child care subsidies, a need for child care must be documented. A parent must show proof that he or she is employed, seeking employment or enrolled in a job training program. Need may also be based on the physical or mental disabilities of a parent.

The demand for subsidized child care far exceeds the funds available, so priorities for services have been established in most states.

Children in danger of abuse or neglect are given first priority and need not be income eligible.

GENERAL CHILD CARE PROGRAMS: General child care programs are usually the largest publicly subsidized child care programs in each state. They provide for the growth and development of children while their parents are working or being trained for a job. General child care programs are often run by public agencies, such as school districts or county education offices. Most of the programs run by public agencies are center-based. Some general child care programs are operated through private agencies, such as local community action organizations or nonprofit corporations. General child care programs provide up to ten hours of care, five days a week.

CAMPUS CHILD DEVELOPMENT PROGRAMS: Campus child care centers provide care for children of students in community colleges, four-year colleges and universities. Care may be given all day or may be adjusted to a parent's class schedule. Centers sometimes serve as training sites for students of the college's child development classes. Programs are funded by a combination of parent fees, student body fees and some state and federal money.

MIGRANT CHILD CARE: Child care for the children of migrant workers is available during peak agricultural periods in most southwestern states and other states with large migrant farm worker industries. Centers offering this child care are operated by county offices, school districts and private nonprofit agencies. Some states also have federally funded and operated migrant child care centers.

SCHOOL-AGE PARENTING AND INFANT DEVELOPMENT: School-age parenting and infant development programs provide child care for infants of high school parents. These programs also provide parenting education and counseling for the school-age parents while they finish high school. These programs are operated by public high schools and are located on or near high school campuses. There is usually no income eligibility requirement for these programs.

SPECIAL PROGRAMS FOR THE HANDICAPPED: Special programs for the severely handicapped provide supervision, therapy, youth guidance and parental counseling to eligible families served by contracting agencies. The federal government also provides some funds for infant and preschool programs for the handicapped.

STATE PRESCHOOLS: State preschool programs provide part-day developmental programs for three-to-five-year-old children from low income families. The preschools offer educational and social services and health and nutrition programs. The preschools emphasize parental education and involvement. Often the children and parents participating in state preschools speak limited English; therefore, in some areas programs have bilingual components. State preschools are administered by school districts, county offices of education and private agencies.

ALTERNATIVE PAYMENT: Child care and child development programs offer an array of alternative payment arrangements. Monthly payments are made to the child care provider selected by the family.

PROTECTIVE SERVICES: These programs are operated through local resources and referral agencies. They provide temporary, emergency child care to children who are in need of protective services due to abuse, neglect or abandonment and who are ineligible for other funds.

SCHOOL-AGE COMMUNITY CHILD CARE SERVICES: These programs provide extended-day programs in a safe environment for school-age children during the hours immediately before and after school. These programs are operated by school districts and nonprofit organizations. At least half of all program costs are usually paid for through parent fees.

HEAD START: Head Start programs are federally funded preschool programs with educational components for children of low income, disadvantaged families. They are mostly part-day programs that operate during the school year (September-June). Parent participation is required. Head Start is similar to most state preschool programs. In some states, Head Start and state preschool programs are combined.

CO-OPS: State subsidized child care co-ops are programs for three-and four-year-old children whose parents are enrolled in adult education classes. There is no income eligibility requirement in most cases. Programs are paid for by parent fees and are subsidized by state and federal funds, usually through the adult education program.

INDIRECT SUBSIDIES FOR CHILD CARE

There are a number of ways the government indirectly subsidizes the cost of child care in the United States. You should check with your local school district or welfare department.

STATE CHILD CARE TAX CREDIT: Most states allow an employer a tax credit for the cost incurred, not to exceed a certain amount, for contributions to a qualified child care plan on behalf of a dependent of an employee who is under a certain age. Most states also offer this credit for start-up expenses of establishing a child care program or constructing a child care facility for its employees.

FEDERAL CHILD CARE TAX CREDIT: The Federal Child Care Tax Credit allows parents to claim a percentage of their child care expenses as a credit on income tax statements. Federal legislation (the Economic Recovery Tax Act of 1988) provides for child care tax credits on a sliding fee scale. The federal credit is nonrefundable, so only those families with enough income to have a tax liability can take advantage of it. There are provisions in the law for advance payment of the tax credit. If eligible for the advance payment, less federal taxes would be taken out of a worker's paycheck, leaving more money with which to purchase child care.

PRIVATE CHILD CARE

Private child care plans are voluntary plans set-up to assist parents with budgetary concerns or special child care needs for handicapped children. You should be aware of the state and federal requirements for in-house care.

SALARY SET-ASIDE PLANS: Set-aside plans allow employers to apply part of an employee's salary toward the employee's child care costs. The employer must set up a Dependent Care Assistance Program (DCAP) which establishes a mechanism for offering child care as a tax-free benefit to employees. The employee may then pay for child care out of pre-tax dollars. State employees are authorized to participate in such plans pursuant to government code. For further information on either child care tax credits or salary set-aside programs, you may want to consult a tax specialist.

IN-HOME CHILD CARE: In-home child care is care for children in their own home. It may involve paid or unpaid care by a relative, friend, housekeeper, nanny or aupair. Such care is usually paid for by the parent. State and federal employment laws are generally applicable to most providers of in-home child care.

FAMILY DAY CARE: Family day care is care for children in homes other than their own. State laws require family day care homes to be licensed through the county.

PRIVATE CHILD CARE CENTERS: Private child care centers are sometimes called "nursery schools" or "preschools." They include church-related programs and parent co-ops. These centers are operated with private funds, usually with fees and/or donations collected from parents. Services are available to children from infancy through school age. Some private centers include kindergartens and some operate separate elementary schools starting with kindergarten so that children can attend school and have child care at the same location. Programs are full day, part day or a combination. A few require parent participation.

WORK SITE CHILD CARE

Work site child care is located at the parent's place of work, but there is not necessarily a commitment of resources from the employer. Space may be rented and the program operated by parents, organizations or unions. Most states have a number of public work site child care facilities available to state workers.

There is an almost overwhelming number of possible child care options. You should assess your own needs and financial abilities in order to choose the child care option that best suits you and your family. Contact your area child care resource and referral agency to find quality child care near you.

CHAPTER 10

RAPE AND OTHER VIOLENT CRIMES

This chapter deals with crimes of violence against women and children. Specifically, it concentrates on sexual assault, wife beating and child abuse. This chapter discusses the legal definitions of each of these violent acts, and gives information on the legal, medical and counseling resources available to survivors of such abuse.

Rape is one of the most dehumanizing crimes of violence. The outrage one experiences with rape is often compounded by other violent, sexual assault types of crime, such as forced oral copulation, forced sodomy and rape by instrumentality. This chapter discusses the laws defining rape, including rape by a spouse, and other forms of sexual assault. It details legal procedures a victim of sexual assault may take, and describes medical and counseling services available to rape victims. Also included is a list of precautions for safety at home and on the street to help women try to reduce the risk of rape and other forms of sexual assault.

Rape statues legislate against sexual intercourse with victims the law views as incapable of giving valid consent. Persons who are underage, mentally defective or incapacitated, unconscious, under the influence of alcohol and drugs, or physically helpless are not assumed to be able to give reasoned consent to sexual intercourse. Willingness does not constitute a defense against the charge that intercourse with such a person is not a form of rape.

Many people have the wrong idea about sexual assault. They mistakenly believe that rapists are overcome with sexual desire or that a woman who is raped may have "dressed seductively" or "asked for it" in some manner. These ideas assume that rape is only a sexual act, a crime that is motivated by desire. It is not. Rape is a violent crime, a hostile act and an attempt to hurt and humiliate another person. Sex is used as a weapon, and rapists use that weapon against women, strangers and acquaintances of all ages, races and body types. No one asks to be raped.

Women are attacked by men in the vast majority in incidents of sexual assault involving an adult man and woman. Most men who are sexually assaulted are assaulted by other men. A proportionally small number of sexual assaults involve a woman attacking a man or another woman. Therefore, this section primarily addresses the issues of women being attacked by men. However, most of the information in this section is applicable to all forms of sexual assault, regardless of the gender of the assailant or victim.

IF YOU ARE ATTACKED

Literature differs on the best way to protect yourself during an assault. All agree, however, that the first thing to do is TRY TO GET AWAY—SCREAM, BLOW A WHISTLE, MAKE NOISE, RUN TO SOME PLACE WHERE THERE ARE PEOPLE OR WHERE YOU WILL BE SAFE. If you are unable to get away immediately, try to stay calm until you can find an opportunity to escape. Be familiar with your limitations. Do not resist a man with a knife, gun or other weapon. Do not worry about "winning," worry about staying alive and getting away.

ACTIVE RESISTANCE: If, by using your body as a weapon, you decide you can escape, try to do it. Self-defense experts warn that you must actually disable your attacker, not merely cause him pain, if you want to escape from him. Aim for his sensitive areas — eyes, nose, groin. Your teeth, arms, feet, fingernails and fists can be effective weapons. Avoid other weapons—weapons you carry yourself can be taken away from you and used against you.

PASSIVE RESISTANCE: If you are unable to escape and afraid to resist by fighting back or screaming, a more passive type of resistance may defuse the violence of the attacker. There are several things you can do:

- Try to calm the attacker. Talk to him and try to persuade him not to carry out the attack. If you win his confidence, you may be able to escape.

- Claim to be sick or pregnant. Tell him you have VD, AIDS or herpes. This may deter the attacker.
- If possible, vomit to repel your attacker.
- Try to discourage the rapist. Some women pretend to faint, some cry hysterically, others act insane or mentally incapacitated.
- If you are at home, tell the attacker that you are expecting someone—a boyfriend, husband or friend.

Remember: There is no single right way to stop an attack. Try to do what you can, but the most important thing is to survive.

LEGAL DEFINITIONS OF SEXUAL ASSAULT

RAPE: "Rape," which is a felony, is defined as an act of sexual intercourse, including sexual penetration, no matter how slight, with a person who is not the spouse of the rapist, under any of the following circumstances:

- Where it is accomplished against a person's will by means of force or threat of immediate bodily injury to the victim or another person.
- Where it is accomplished by the rapist threatening to retaliate in the future against the victim or anyone else, and there is a reasonable possibility that the rapist will carry out the threat. Threatening to retaliate means a threat to kidnap or falsely imprison or to inflict extreme pain, serious bodily injury or death.
- Where a person is incapable of giving legal consent because of a mental disorder or developmental or physical disability and the rapist knows or should know it.
- Where a person is prevented from resisting because the rapist caused her to be drugged or intoxicated.
- Where the person is unconscious of the nature of the act and the rapist knows it.
- Where the person submits under the mistaken belief that the rapist is her spouse and the rapist intentionally induced that belief.

- Where it is accomplished against a person's will by threatening to use the authority of a public official to incarcerate, arrest or deport the person, and the person has a reasonable belief that the perpetrator is a public official. The perpetrator does not actually have to be a public official.

RAPE BY A SPOUSE: Rape by a spouse is a crime in some states. However in nine states—Alabama, Arkansas, Kansas, Montana, South Dakota, Texas, Vermont, Washington and West Virginia—husbands are immune from marital rape prosecutions. In twenty-six others, they can be convicted only in very narrow circumstances, generally when the partners are living apart under court order or legally separated. In Alaska and Washington a man can rape his wife legally if she is mentally incapable and he is her legal guardian. Marital rape laws are being changed in many states. Some of the newest changes are:

- The repeal of all exemptions for rape prosecution for husbands in New Mexico and Utah.
- The repeal of most exemptions for husbands in Missouri and Texas.
- The repeal of some exemptions for husbands in South Carolina.
- The repeal of all exemptions from cohabitant and date rape in Montana.

In twelve states, the exemption from prosecution for marital rape has been expanded to cover unmarried couples. A man who rapes the woman he is living with but to whom he is not legally married cannot be charged with rape in these jurisdictions. "Spousal rape" is defined as an act of sexual intercourse accomplished against the will of the other spouse by means of force or fear of immediate bodily injury to the spouse or another, or where the rape is accomplished by threatening to retaliate in the future against the spouse or any other person, and there is a reasonable possibility that the rapist will execute the threat. As with the general definition of rape, the word "retaliation" means a threat by the rapist to kidnap or falsely imprison, or to inflict extreme pain, serious bodily injury or death.

In order to have a spouse arrested or prosecuted for rape, the spousal victim must report the rape to the police or district attorney usually within ninety days after the rape.

RAPE BY A FOREIGN DEVICE OR INSTRUMENT: It is unlawful to force even the slightest penetration of the genital or anal opening of another person by any foreign object, instrument, substance, device or bodily part (other than a sexual organ) or to cause another person to do so for the purpose of sexual arousal, gratification or abuse under all of the circumstances which cause sexual penetration to be rape.

FORCED ORAL COPULATION: Forced oral copulation is a crime. Oral copulation is the placing of the mouth of one person on the sexual organs or anus of another person or by assisting some-one else to do so. It is a crime under all of the circumstances which cause sexual penetration to be rape.

FORCED SODOMY: Forced sodomy is a crime. A person is guilty of the crime of sodomy if he uses his penis to penetrate the anus of another person under all of the circumstances which cause sexual penetration to be rape.

STATUTORY RAPE: Statutory rape is the rape of a person below a certain age. In most states, the statutory age is somewhere between twelve and sixteen years of age. Typically, only men can be charged with statutory rape, but some states have laws which also prohibit this type of rape by women.

ATTEMPTED ASSAULT WITH INTENT TO COMMIT RAPE: Attempted assault with intent to commit rape, rape by in-strumentality, forced sodomy or forced oral copulation are illegal.

SEXUAL BATTERY: Sexual battery is a crime. A person is guilty of sexual battery if he touches the intimate parts (sexual organ, anus, groin, buttocks of any person, and breasts of a woman), either directly or through the person's clothing or caused that person to masturbate or touch the intimate parts of another where:

- The victim is unlawfully restrained by the accused or by an accomplice, and if the touching was against the victim's will, for the purpose of sexual arousal, gratification or abuse.
- The victim is institutionalized for medical treatment and is seriously disabled or medically incapacitated, if the touching is against the victim's will and for the purpose of sexual arousal, gratification or abuse.

WHAT YOU CAN DO IF YOU ARE SEXUALLY ASSAULTED

Many women are initially overwhelmed at the prospect of facing the medical and legal procedures which follow a rape. Rapists know this and hope their victims will not report the crime. However, often victims who do report the rape feel stronger by taking positive action to aid law enforcement officers in capturing and prosecuting the rapist. Nonetheless, if you feel you are unable to report the rape to the police, you should take steps to protect your own mental and physical well-being and that of other potential victims.

STALKING

Any person who willfully, maliciously and repeatedly follows or harasses another person and who makes a credible threat with the intent to place that person in reasonable fear of death or great bodily injury or to place that person in reasonable fear of the death or great bodily injury of his or her immediate family is guilty of the crime of stalking in most states.

Any person who violates an injunction, when there is a temporary restraining order, or any other court order in effect prohibiting the behavior described against the same party, is punishable by imprisonment in a county jail, a fine or both a fine and imprisonment.

If after having been convicted of a stalking violation, a person has a second or subsequent conviction (occurring within seven years against the same victim and involving an act of violence or a credible threat of violence) the second conviction is punishable by imprisonment in a state prison.

THE POLICE

If you are sexually assaulted, you can call the police and receive immediate assistance. Statistics show that rapists repeat their crimes, so by calling the police after a rape, you may help catch and imprison a rapist before he rapes someone else. When you call the police emergency number (911) and report that you have been raped, you can expect to be asked the following questions by the police dispatcher over the phone:

- Your name and location.
- Whether you need emergency medical assistance.
- How long ago the assault occurred.
- A brief description of the rapist, his car or other form of transportation, and the direction he was last seen traveling.
- If the rapist had a weapon. This is for the officers' safety, in case of an immediate apprehension, and your own future safety.

If you feel that it would be easier for you to discuss the attack with a woman, ask the police to send a woman investigator to see you. In most states, law enforcement agencies will try to provide a female officer for a rape victim upon request. You may also be able to have a friend, relative or counselor from a rape crisis center accompany you during the police interviews.

The police departments of most cities with large ethnic populations have bilingual police officers available to send to your location to talk to you. Be sure to ask for a bilingual officer if you want one.

Police officers will ask you only general questions about the attack unless you want to make a complete statement at that time. They will gather as much evidence as they can. As part of a follow-up investigation, a police investigator will be assigned to your case to collect evidence and work with you to try to arrest the man who assaulted you. You may request that one of the investigators on your case be a woman. You will be asked to describe the attack and your assailant in detail. In most cases, you do not have to discuss your past sexual history. You do have to discuss past sexual relations you may have had with the man who raped you. In most states, you should not be asked if you enjoyed the assault or had an orgasm. You have a right to ask the officers to explain why they are asking you certain questions. You may be asked to view pictures (mug shots) of several men to try to identify the man who raped you. In most states the police cannot ask you to take a polygraph test (lie detector test).

MEDICAL HELP

It is very important that you get immediate medical care. Even if you cannot see any visible signs of injury, you may be suffering from serious internal injuries. Also, you may have contracted a venereal disease from the rapist or you may be pregnant. Currently, AIDS tests involve testing for the AIDS antibody which may not appear until three months after infection. Therefore, if you are worried that you may have contracted AIDS from your assailant, you may want to have an AIDS test done a few months after being sexually assaulted. However, there are no known AIDS cases among women which were transmitted through a single, forced, heterosexual encounter.

Many states have new laws that permit you to request that your assailant be given an AIDS antibody test. The test may have to be approved by the suspect before the AIDS antibody test can be given but you should ask anyway. Also, many states now require a defendant in a rape case to be tested for the AIDS antibody although the results may not be used in court. Again, there are no known cases of AIDS among women which were transmitted as the result of a single, forced, heterosexual encounter. The results of a blood test pursuant to penal code cannot be used in any criminal or juvenile proceeding in most cases as evidence of either guilt or innocence.

It is also important that you get immediate medical care because valuable medical evidence should be collected within twelve hours of the assault, although it can be collected up to seventy-two hours after the attack. You do not have to give the medical personnel all of the details of the assault. However, you do have to say you were sexually assaulted in order to receive proper treatment. Even if you decide not to make a police report, the doctor treating you will collect all possible evidence in case you later change your mind. You do not have to consent to an examination for evidence of sexual assault.

If you report the rape to the police and they take you to the hospital or make arrangements to meet you there before the examination, the police department, county or local government agency will pay all or most of the expenses for the medical tests needed for legal evidence in almost every case.

Other expenses, such as major medical or hospitalization costs, wages lost from inability to work and psychological counseling may be reimbursed by filing for reimbursement under the Aid to Victims of Violent Crimes Act.

You should not wash yourself or your clothes before going for medical treatment. Your first instinct after being raped might be to clean yourself completely and to wash away the entire incident. DO NOT DO THIS. Washing your body may remove vital evidence needed for possible conviction of your assailant. While waiting for the police and a counselor from a crisis center to arrive:

- Do not wash any part of your body including your mouth, and do not douche.
- Do not change your clothes. If you feel you must change your clothes, place each item of clothing you remove in a separate bag.
- Do not clean or straighten your house or any other area that was the scene of the assault.
- Do not destroy or discard your clothing, your underclothes, or sheets and towels you may have used. These items could contain valuable evidence.

You are not required to make a police report to receive emergency medical treatment in most cases. But, in most states, every physician and hospital is required by law to report the name, address, type of assault, nature and extent of injury of each victim of a violent crime that they treat. This does not mean that a formal police report is filed. The police cannot take action on your case until you report the rape.

You may be able to have a person of your choice present during the medical examination. This person can be a friend or an advocate from a rape crisis center.

You will undergo a general physical examination (blood pressure, weight, temperature, ears, eyes, mouth, hearing, etc.) a pelvic examination (external pelvic and internal genital) and tests for venereal disease and pregnancy. The doctor may offer you the "morning after pill" (diethylstilbestrol-DES) to terminate a possible pregnancy, however, you should inquire as to the possible side affects from DES.

The doctor or police may want to take pictures of your injuries as evidence. They will usually want to wait twenty-four hours in order for the full effect of the bruises to develop. You can decide who will take the pictures—a social worker, rape crisis advocate, doctor, nurse or police officer.

You will be asked to sign a release of evidence form, consent forms, police reports, etc. If you do not understand what is in the documents, you should ask to have them explained to you. Do not be afraid to ask questions. You have a right to know what you are signing.

RAPE CRISIS CENTERS

Rape crisis centers are organizations which help women who have been victims of rape or other violent crimes to get medical assistance and counseling to help cope with the emotional and physical trauma they experience. You can get the name and phone number of the rape crisis center or similar organization in your area from the police, emergency hospital or your local directory assistance operator.

When you call the rape crisis center, tell them what happened to you. These centers generally provide twenty-four-hour telephone counseling, as well as in-person counseling and referral services during normal business hours. Their services are generally free to rape victims. Most centers also provide victims with counselors or advocates who will accompany a rape victim during police interviews, medical examinations and court proceedings. You have a right to be accompanied by either a friend, relative or counselor from a rape crisis center during court proceedings.

If you do not want to report the rape to the police, a rape crisis center can do it for you without involving you specifically. That way the police can be alerted to the presence of a rapist in your area.

You do not need to have been raped recently to call a rape crisis center, nor do you need to be a woman. Most rape crisis centers offer support services to all survivors of sexual assault, female and male victims, and often to a survivor's spouse, partner or lover as well.

THE LEGAL PROCESS

A prosecuting attorney in the District Attorney's Office will be assigned to review your case. The attorney can explain the legal procedures for prosecution to you and will tell you what testimony you would be required to give and how often you might have to appear in court. Counselors and lawyers with rape crisis centers and victim's witness assistance programs can also explain legal procedures to you.

If you were attacked by your spouse or someone you know, you can have a temporary restraining order issued if you are afraid your assailant will continue to harass you.

IF THE SUSPECT IS ARRESTED: If your attacker is arrested, the deputy district attorney will decide whether to issue a formal complaint against him. This decision is based on the strength of the evidence against the suspect.

The suspected rapist has a right to a defense attorney during all legal actions. The suspect may be assigned an attorney from the Public Defender's Office to represent him on the case. The public defender may also assign an investigator to work on the case.

You are not obligated to speak with the defense attorney or his or her investigator, or anyone else about your case until you are in court. If you choose to answer an attorney's or investigator's questions, you may have another person present with you if you wish. You should also notify the deputy district attorney. You should always ask for identification and an explanation of the purpose from anyone contacting you about the case.

IF THE SUSPECT IS CHARGED WITH RAPE: Once the suspect is formally charged, he is called a "defendant." Before the actual trial, the court conducts a hearing, called a "preliminary hearing," to determine whether the prosecutor has enough evidence to show that the rape was committed and that the defendant is probably the one who committed the rape so that he may be tried for the rape.

You will be subpoenaed to appear at the preliminary hearing. At the preliminary hearing, you are a witness for the prosecution. You are not on trial. The deputy district attorney prosecutes the case on behalf of the people of the state in which the rape was committed, and not on behalf of you directly, because a rape, like any other violent crime, is considered a crime against the state.

You have a right to have a person of your choosing at this hearing to provide you with moral support. The person need not be a witness in the case.

At both the preliminary hearing and trial, you will be questioned by the deputy district attorney and the defendant's attorney. They will be able to ask you about any prior sexual relations you may have had with the defendant (over half of all rapes are committed by a man known to the victim). However, they will not be able to ask you questions about your sexual conduct with persons other than the defendant (in most states, but not all) in order to try to prove you consented to the defendant's acts. Your prior sexual history is almost always considered irrelevant and rarely will a judge allow you to be questioned about it.

After the evidence is heard at the preliminary hearing, the judge will decide whether to send the case to Superior Court for a trial. I the judge does not believe there is enough evidence, the charges will be dropped and the suspect will be released.

THE TRIAL: If there is a trial, it may take place several months after the rape. The prosecutor will contact you to prepare you for trial.

At the trial, if the defense attorney has asked that witnesses be excluded from the courtroom, witnesses are permitted in the courtroom only when they are testifying.

You may ask the district attorney to request that you be allowed not to give your address and telephone number when you testify. In addition, you have a right to bring friends, relatives or other supportive people with you to the trial.

In most states, the defendant's attorney cannot order you to submit to a psychiatric examination for the purpose of measuring your credibility.

If the defendant is found not guilty, he will be released immediately. A finding of not guilty means that there was not enough evidence for the jury or the judge, if it was not a jury trial, to believe that the rapist was guilty "beyond a reasonable doubt."

If the defendant is convicted, he will be sentenced approximately thirty days later at a sentencing hearing.

After the trial, the deputy district attorney should call you and tell you the outcome of the case and what will happen to the defendant.

If the defendant is convicted, you may be contacted by a probation officer so that your comments about the rapist can be reported to the judge at the time of sentencing. If you desire, you or your parent or guardian, if you are a minor, may be allowed to testify in person at the sentencing hearing.

PRECAUTIONS

Unfortunately, no one can prevent a rape, but listed below are some general precautions women can take to reduce the risk of being a victim of rape or another violent crime. If you are a victim of rape or other violent crime, there are people to help you.

AT HOME: The following are ways to protect yourself
home:

- Keep all exterior doors and windows securely locked.
- All entrances and hallways should be well lighted.
- Hang curtains and or blinds on all windows.
- Be aware of places attackers might hide, both inside and outside.
- NEVER open the door to a stranger. Install a peephole i your front door.
- If you live alone or with other women, don't list your full name on your mailbox or in the telephone book, use your first initial only.
- Avoid publicizing that you live alone.
- Let a friend know when you leave and when you plan to return, so that someone will be aware if you are missing.
- Keep your garage locked.
- Leave a light on when you go out.
- When you return home, if there are any signs of an intruder or forced entry, seek help. DO NOT ENTER ALONE.
- Take a self-defense class. There are many self-defense classes designed for women.

ON THE STREET: The following are ways to protect you
self while walking or driving on the street:

- Walk in well-lighted areas.
- Avoid walking alone.
- Walk at a steady pace, look confident and purposeful. Know where you are going. Do not look lost.
- Be familiar with your own frequently used route. Vary your route home.
- Try to keep your hands free.
- Listen for footsteps and voices nearby. Be alert to discover if someone is following you. If you think someone is following you, cross the street or walk in the middle of

the street. Stay near street lights or go into a store or office where people are working.

⊛ If you fear danger, scream loudly or yell "fire." (Fire is a threat to which almost everyone will respond.) Get to a lighted place fast. Run and yell!

• Carry a whistle wrapped around your wrist or on your key chain. Use it!

• If you are waiting outside, stand in a balanced position. Be suspicious of cars that pull up near you or keep passing you.

• If a car is following you, turn around and walk in the reverse direction.

• Dress for freedom of movement. Wear sensible shoes that allow you to run.

• Walk on the outside of the sidewalk, away from possible hiding places.

• Have your car key out and ready to use when you go to your parked car.

• Check the interior of your car before you get in. Always keep car doors locked when parked and when driving.

• Always carry enough money for an emergency whenever you go out.

• Carry a flare in your car for emergencies.

• Drive to a police station if you are threatened while in your car.

• Again, take a self-defense class.

WHEN HITCHHIKING: Avoid hitchhiking whenever possible. Arrange a ride with a friend, borrow a friend's car, use public transportation or join a car pool. If you must hitchhike:

• Try to get a ride with a woman.

• Avoid hitchhiking alone.

• Check the license plate number and write it down before getting into the car.

• Check to see that no one is hiding in the car and that the driver is the only occupant.

- Become familiar with the vehicle make, model, color, etc.
- Be sure the door handle on the passenger's side works before getting in.
- Do not get in the car of someone who you think has been drinking.
- Do not get in the back of a van or a two-door car.
- Ask the driver's destination and determine if it is where you want to go.
- Try to make sure it is a safe ride before putting any of your possessions into the car or trunk.
- Look closely at the driver so you can later identify him or her.
- Do not talk openly about yourself or give your home address or telephone number.
- Do not allow the driver to take you to your home, get out of the car at least a block away.
- Hitchhike in an area where there is ample pull-off space.
- If you feel uncomfortable abut the situation, do not get into the car.
- Again, take a self-defense class.

ACQUAINTANCES: It has been estimated that in over hal of all cases of sexual assault, the rapist is an acquaintance of hi victim. So, you need to be cautious even with people you know.

- Do not assume that you are safe solely because you are with someone you know.
- Consider having dates, especially first and second dates, take place in public places.
- Trust your instincts. If you feel uncomfortable in a situation, do something about it.
- Remember you have a right to say NO to unwanted sexua advances.

THE PSYCHOLOGICAL IMPACT OF RAPE

Most rape victims suffer physical and emotional reactions that continue for months after the rape occurred. Rape counselors have noted two stages of the "rape trauma syndrome" that affect most rape victims. In the first stage (lasting anywhere from one week to three months), victims often feel loss of control, shame, fear of dying, physical pain, inability to sleep, depression and other symptoms of severe trauma. The second stage, or reorganization phase, may last a year or longer. It is often characterized by minor or major adjustments in lifestyle which are motivated by fear (changing jobs, quitting school, moving, etc.). Many rape victims have been helped by mental health professionals and counselors to overcome most of their negative symptoms and reactions after a rape. It is important for any victim of a rape or other violent crime to seek all available help.

It is recommended that a victim:

- Report the rape to the police.
- Call a rape crisis center.
- Get medical attention.
- Call a mental health professional or county mental health facility.
- Try to surround herself or himself with supportive friends and family.
- Find out if he or she qualifies for state financial assistance as a victim of violent crime under the Aid to Victims of Violent Crimes Act.

CHAPTER 11

DOMESTIC VIOLENCE

Domestic violence is a major problem in the United States. An estimated one-fourth of all murders in this country occur within the family, and one-half of these are husband-wife killings.

What is "Domestic Violence?" It is generally defined as all forms of violent behavior between people who live together. Domestic violence includes a husband who beats his wife, a wife who beats her husband, an unmarried person who is beaten by the person with whom he or she lives, and a parent, guardian or other family member who sexually assaults or physically abuses a child in the family (also included are elderly parents beaten by their children or grandchildren).

In all states, it is a crime for any person to beat or sexually assault another person. In some states, these crimes are generally called "assaults or batteries" and may be punished as misdemeanors and felonies as provided by law.

Many states now recognize that a spouse can commit rape against his or her spouse. Under some state laws, a spouse commits rape against his spouse if he accomplishes an act of sexual intercourse with her, against her will, by means of force or fear, or by threatening immediate and unlawful bodily injury on his spouse or another. Some states also recognize as rape an act of sexual intercourse accomplished against the victim's will by threatening to retaliate in the future against the victim or any other person when there is a reasonable possibility that the threat will be executed. To arrest or prosecute your husband for raping you, you must report the rape to the police or the district attorney within the period of time designated by the laws of the state where the rape occurred.

In nine states - Alabama, Arkansas, Kansas, Montana, South Dakota, Texas, Vermont, Washington and West Virginia - husbands are immune from marital rape prosecutions. In twenty-six others they can be convicted only in very narrow circumstances, generally when the partners are living apart under court order or legally separated. In twelve states, the exemption from prosecution for marital rape has been expanded to cover unmarried couples. A man who rapes the woman he is living with but to whom he is not legally married cannot be charged with rape in these jurisdictions. This area of the law, because of actions by women's rights groups, is now being changed in many states. States with existing marital rape laws are creating new, more stringent laws with regard to marital rape, and states without marital rape laws are in the process of reviewing potential laws at this time.

WIFE BEATING

Much of the information in this section applies to victims of both wife beating and child abuse. However, because there are issues that separate the two, they are divided into separate sections. (The term "wife beating" also refer to the beating of a person of the opposite sex with whom one lives or who is the parent of one's child.)

Also, this section focuses on women who are battered by their husbands because that is the norm. However, it is not unheard of for wives to abuse their husbands or for one partner in a non-marital relationship to physically abuse the other. Much of the information in this section is relevant to any case of domestic abuse.

WHAT TO DO IF YOUR HUSBAND BEATS YOU (OR YOUR CHILDREN): If your husband beats you or your children, you should:

- Make sure you are safe from another beating. Call friends, relatives, neighbors or a battered women's shelter to help you.
- Call the police immediately. The police are obligated to protect you and arrest your attacker. If a police officer does not arrive within a few minutes, call again.
- When the police arrive, insist on filing a police report whether or not you intend to press charges.

- Write down the officer's name and badge number.
- If the police arrest your husband, he will probably be released in a short period of time. Take immediate steps to protect yourself and your children from future abuse.
- Save all the evidence of what happened to you. Save the clothing you were wearing when you were attacked. Tak color pictures of your injuries. If you required medical at tention, get a copy of the medical record. Ask for a copy of the police report.
- Call a shelter for battered women. Tell the counselor exactly what has happened to you. Most emergency shelter for battered women keep the shelter address a secret so that an attacker cannot find a woman who goes to the shelter. A person from the shelter may be able to arrange to meet you and your children at a neutral place to take you to the shelter. You will be asked to keep the address of the shelter confidential. If the shelter is full, however, you will need to consider other resources for housing such as friends or family.

YOUR RIGHTS IF YOU HAVE BEEN ATTACKED: You have a right to defend yourself. However, the force you use must b only enough to stop the attacker. If you use greater force than th law feels is necessary, you may be accused of attacking your hus band. It is important that you know that some women who have killed their husbands, reportedly in response to domestic violence have been convicted of murder and sent to prison.

You can get a temporary restraining order if you fear an attack The court can issue a temporary restraining order to your husband or the man you are living with, ordering him to stay away from you and/or your children or to move out.

If necessary, through the police you can get an emergency pro tective order by telephone when courts are not in session, such as on nights and weekends, to protect you from abuse by a family mem ber until the second court day after the incident.

You may get a temporary restraining order even if you have not filed for divorce or you have not separated from your husband or the man with whom you are living. You will probably have to show the court that there have been recent instances of physical abuse against you. You can get such an order by filling out forms available at the county court. If you have an attorney, he or she can help you get such an order, or call a battered women's shelter for help.

The court also may determine who will have temporary possession of property that you own together and determine temporary custody of your children.

Also, the court may issue an order requiring both parties to attend at least one counseling session with a family counselor of the parties' mutual choice.

If you are filing for dissolution of marriage (divorce) and custody of your children, you can ask for a temporary restraining order at the same time that you file for dissolution.

If you get a temporary restraining order, make sure your attacker, the police department and court receive a copy. This order must include a proof of service. Do not deliver it to your attacker yourself. Any law officer who is present at the scene of the domestic violence can serve this order. If your attacker does not obey the order, report it to the police. These orders may be good for up to three years.

If you own or rent your home or apartment with your attacker, you may not refuse to let him in without a restraining order signed by a judge. However, if you believe you are in imminent danger of an attack, call the police for assistance before allowing your co-owner or co-renter to enter. If you own or rent by yourself or have a restraining order, you may keep him out and/or ask him to leave. If he refuses, call the police and ask that he be arrested for trespassing.

FINANCIAL ASSISTANCE: Some states provide compensation to victims of violent crime, their dependents, family members or persons in close relationship with the victim, if they suffer serious financial loss. A higher amount may be payable if matching federal funds are available. Coverage may include necessary medical expenses, lost earnings, child care, counseling and costs of job retraining. Attorneys' fees may also be available.

To receive state compensation, you must have suffered physical or emotional injury as a result of a violent crime. Generally, you must have been a state resident when the crime occurred, or be military personnel or family of military personnel stationed in the state where the criminal acts occurred. Non-residents of a state who suffer monetary losses as a result of a criminal act may also be compensated if federal funds are available. Emergency awards may also be made if the victim incurs loss of income. Most state programs do not allow compensation to victims who are married to or living with their assailant because the assailant might indirectly receive the compensation and benefit from his crime. Some states, however, allow compensation to victims who live with the assailant, usually the assailant must be receiving therapy. In cases of the victim's death, the heirs may have rights to this compensation for financial losses to the deceased.

A victim of any crime, including domestic violence, may not receive compensation if she refuses to cooperate with the police in apprehending and prosecuting the assailant, or if she is a convicted felon who has not yet been discharged from parole or probation, or if she knowingly and willingly participates in committing the crime.

PRESSING CHARGES: When the police arrive, insist on filing a police report, even if you do not want to press charges and no arrest is made. The police report is crucial for your future protection. In some cases, you will not have to press charges as the crime committed may be a felony whose statute requires arrest of the person suspected of committing the crime. The report is important if you ever want to press charges. It will support you if you are attacked again and want to press charges, seek to gain custody of your children or wish to obtain a temporary restraining order against your husband.

YOU CAN HAVE YOUR ATTACKER ARRESTED: There are two ways for you to have your attacker arrested: police arrest and citizen's arrest. Also, the police may issue a misdemeanor citation against your attacker in less serious situations.

POLICE ARREST: When the police answer your call, you must tell them if you want your attacker arrested. Police are often reluctant to make an arrest in domestic violence situations, so be very clear as to your desires. The police can only arrest the attacker if he commits a crime in their presence or if they have reasonable cause to believe that a serious attack (felony) has been committed. Felonies are more serious attacks and threats, while misdemeanors are less serious. To help the police decide whether a felony has been committed and whether to arrest the attacker, you should:
- Describe the attack to them, telling them the amount of force used.
- Describe your injuries.
- Tell the police if a weapon was used or threatened to be used against you. A marshal or deputy marshal, at the scene of an incident of domestic violence involving a threat to human life or physical assault, has the authority to temporarily take custody of any firearm in plain sight or discovered pursuant to a consensual search.

A police officer has a duty to listen to your statement and to make a police report. You may take the name and badge number of the officer for your own record. You may ask for the police officer's superior to be present if you think you are having a problem with the officer on the scene.

CITIZEN'S ARREST: If your attacker was not arrested and you have decided to press charges, you must file a police report. The police will then go to the District Attorney's Office with a copy of this report, (in some locations, misdemeanors are prosecuted by the city attorney instead of the district attorney). To proceed, the district attorney must be convinced that a crime probably was committed and that the person accused probably committed it. If you have any evidence of the crime, you should give it to the police and request that they take it to the District Attorney's Office. It is helpful to get color photographs of your injuries for use at the trial. To encourage prosecution, you may have to convince the district attorney that you are serious about your decision to press charges and that you will not later withdraw your complaint and refuse to testify. You should telephone the District Attorney's Office and make an appointment to talk with a deputy district attorney. Some District Attorney's Offices have special programs to assist victims of domestic violence. If the district attorney decides to prosecute your attacker for a crime or crimes, the case will go to preliminary hearing and trial.

AFTER AN ARREST: Even if your husband is arrested and taken to the police station, he may be free to return home in a short period of time after his arrest. The police may issue a misdemeanor citation (similar to a traffic ticket) and let him go. At most, a few hours after he is taken to the police station his bail will be set and, if he has money, he can post bail and be released. If he has no money but has friends or relatives who will vouch for him, he may be released on his own recognizance—his promise to return for formal hearing.

In any case, you must be prepared for the possibility that your husband may return soon after he has been arrested. He may return home in an angry, violent mood. On the other hand, the arrest may make him realize how serious his actions were.

If you believe your husband will return home to beat you in revenge, arrange to stay with friends or relatives or call a women's shelter immediately to arrange a safe place for you and your children to stay until you make new plans.

CRIMINAL PROSECUTION

After your attacker is arrested, the police report is sent to the district attorney to draw up a complaint for prosecution. The district attorney may ask you to come to the District Attorney's Office for an interview. If the crime is a felony, the district attorney will sign the complaint. If the crime is a misdemeanor and if there was no police officer at the scene of the beating who saw the crime and can testify as a witness at trial, the district attorney may ask you to sign the misdemeanor complaint.

If a citizen's arrest was made after the beating, you will have to go to the District Attorney's Office the next day to make a formal citizen's complaint. Some district attorneys may be reluctant to prosecute your husband if it appears that you are not firm in your decision to press charges and if you appear unwilling to testify against him.

Once the district attorney has filed a formal criminal complaint on behalf of the state, only the district attorney can withdraw it. In those cases where the victim is the only witness to the attack, it is difficult for the district attorney to proceed without the voluntary cooperation of the victim.

You will be served with a subpoena to testify as a witness in court. Statistics show that a large number of domestic violence victims refuse to testify. Prosecuting a criminal case is time-consuming and costly to the state. Therefore, district attorneys may be reluctant to file complaints if they believe that you will not testify voluntarily. If you are serious about pressing charges and testifying, you should emphasize these intentions to the district attorney to encourage prosecution.

An arraignment will usually be held a few days after the arrest. The arraignment is a hearing before a judge where the defendant is told of the criminal charges against him. Bail will be set at this hearing. You may ask the judge, as a condition of bail, to order your husband to stay away from you. If such an order is issued as a condition of bail, and your husband breaks the order by coming to see you, his bail may be revoked and he could be jailed.

THE TRIAL: First, there may be a preliminary hearing. If the attack was serious enough to be deemed a felony, you will be required to testify at a preliminary hearing. At the preliminary hearing, the district attorney must present enough proof to show that you have been attacked by the suspect. You will have to answer questions from your attacker's attorney. If you are unwilling to testify, the charges may be dropped and the prosecution may end

Whether the case involves a felony or a misdemeanor, you will probably be required to testify against your attacker at trial. At the trial, the district attorney will ask you about your relationship with the attacker, the attacker's personality and treatment of you, the argument or events which preceded the attack, the time and place of the attack, the pain and injuries you suffered and the steps you have taken to protect yourself.

You will be cross-examined by the defense attorney. The defense attorney may challenge the truth of your statements, and may accuse you, rather than the defendant, of being at fault. You may bring friends or relatives to court with you who can give you more support and encouragement. You may also bring staff people from a women's shelter with you.

When you finish testifying and are dismissed from the witness stand, you are free to leave the courthouse. You may wish to do so immediately to avoid seeing the defendant and to prevent him from following you to your home or shelter when the trial is adjourned for the day. If you fear your attacker will be released and then follow you and beat you to get even with you for pressing charges ask the police to escort you safely home.

To find your attacker guilty, the district attorney must convince the judge or the jury that the defendant is guilty beyond a reasonable doubt. If the defendant is found not guilty, he will be released immediately.

ALTERNATIVES TO CRIMINAL PROSECUTION: Recognizing the hardships on victims and families when criminal prosecution is involved, some District Attorney's Offices have set up alternatives to criminal prosecution. Under these alternatives, the attacker is not sent to trial and jail. Instead, efforts are made to help the parties work out their differences through peaceful means to preserve the family.

CITATION HEARING: One of the non-criminal procedures that tries to reconcile disputes instead of punishing the attacker called a "citation hearing." A citation hearing provides a setting where both parties can present their feelings about the reasons for their dispute rather than only presenting evidence about the attack, as they would at a trial. The success of a citation hearing usually depends on the cooperation of the attacker, his recognition of the seriousness of his offense and the desire of both parties to preserve their relationship.

If you believe that the citation procedure is not useful, inform the district attorney of your conclusion and reasons, and emphasize your intention to stand by the prosecution and testify against your attacker.

If the crime was a serious one, if a dangerous weapon was used and/or you were seriously injured, the district attorney will be more willing to prosecute and less likely to suggest the citation procedure. Contact the District Attorney's Office for more information.

PRE-TRIAL DIVERSION PROGRAMS: Some courts and counties have set up special community-based programs that try to rehabilitate violence-prone persons through counseling, psychiatric care, participation in alcohol and drug abuse treatment programs and other programs, such as special treatment programs for people who beat their spouses. In a proper case, usually one involving a minor offense (not a violent crime with severe injury), and usually where there is mutual consent, a judge will allow the defendant (attacker) to participate in a pre-trial diversion program. If the diversion is not successful, the defendant may be tried at a later time for the crime. The defendant must ask for this procedure from the judge after the filing a complaint.

If your attacker is on probation, send a copy of your police report and/or restraining orders to his probation officer. Call the county probation department where your attacker was sentenced to find out who his probation officer is.

If your attacker is on parole, call the Department of Corrections and report the attack to his parole agent. Your attacker may have his parole revoked and be sent back to prison.

If you are afraid of a man who is in a state prison, you can find out when and where he will be released by contacting your local Department of Corrections.

CHAPTER 12

CHILD ABUSE

Child abuse is any act or lack of action which puts a child' physical or emotional health and development in danger. Child abus can take the form of physical abuse, sexual abuse, emotional abuse emotional deprivation, physical neglect or inadequate supervision

CORPORAL PUNISHMENT (SPANKING)

Corporal punishment in some states is illegal. In states where is legal, it may become child abuse. Corporal punishment can be come abusive when a parent, teacher, scoutmaster, adoptive paren or neighbor uses extreme or inappropriate forms of corporal pun ishment. When corporal punishment is administered in an out-of control way, out of anger and frustration, with a high degree o force, or when forms of corporal punishment are used, not in rela tion to the child's developmental age or with objects such as belts cords or brooms, it is child abuse in most states.

THE PENALTY FOR ABUSING OR NEGLECTING A CHILD

Child abuse is a crime. A person convicted of child abuse ca be jailed and fined. It does not matter whether the abusers are par ents who are married or parents who are divorced or separated Any parent is responsible for the physical and emotional health o his or her child.

An abused child can be removed from an unsafe environmen and from an unfit parent or guardian. Usually, any child under the age of eighteen can be placed under the juvenile court's jurisdictior if the child:

- Is in need of proper and effectual parental care or control and has no parent or guardian, or has no parent or guardian willing or capable of exercising such care or control or actually exercising such care or control.

- Is destitute, is not provided with the necessities of life or is not provided with a home or suitable place of abode.
- Has a home which is unfit for him or her because of neglect, cruelty, depravity or physical abuse by his or her parents or guardian.

This means that the court can decide if the child should be made a dependent of the court to protect such a child from more abuse or neglect. A police officer may, without a warrant in most cases, take a child into temporary protective custody. The officer may transport the child either to a hospital or special holding facility with or without parental consent, if abuse is suspected.

If a child is found to be a victim of abuse or neglect, the court will determine what steps should be taken to protect the child. Such steps may include keeping the child at home under the supervision of the local welfare or social services department, or placing the child with relatives, in foster care or in other child care facilities.

WHO TO CONTACT FOR HELP

If your husband, a person you are living with or anyone you know is abusing a child, you should contact one of the following to get help:

- Your local sheriff or police department.
- The child abuse hotline, council or center in your area.
- Parents anonymous.
- The child protective services unit of your local welfare or social services department.

IF YOU NEED HELP TO STOP ABUSING YOUR CHILD

If you as a parent, caretaker, foster parent, guardian or baby sitter and feel that you need help in dealing with the children for whom you are responsible, contact:

- The child abuse hotline, council or center in your area.
- Parents anonymous.

- The child protective services unit of your local welfare or social services department.

WHAT TO DO IF YOU KNOW A CHILD WHO IS BEING ABUSED

If you know or suspect a child is being abused or neglected, immediately call:
- Your local police or county sheriff's department.
- Your County Welfare Department. Other names may be: Human Resources Agency, Department of Public Social Services, Department of Health and Human Services, Department of Public Assistance.
- Your local county juvenile probation department.
- The child abuse and neglect hotline, council or center in your area.

If you do not want to identify yourself, reports may be made anonymously to these agencies. For investigation and follow-ups, it is preferred, but not required, that the name and address of the reporter be volunteered. The most important thing, however, is the immediate protection of the abused child.

IF YOU WERE ABUSED AS A CHILD

Child abuse often leaves lasting scars. What's more, people who were abused as children are more likely to abuse their own children than people who were not abused as children. For your own sake and to help break the cycle, you might want to see a private therapist, or look in your local telephone book for organizations that counsel or sponsor group sessions for survivors of child abuse.

DIRECTORY OF SERVICES AND INFORMATION

This general directory lists various legal assistance agencies, government agencies and other organizations that may be able to provide legal assistance and general information to women on the subjects discussed in this book. This directory is not a complete list of every women's organization in the country. Many of the organizations listed here may be able to direct you to another organization that can help you with specific problems.

It may be helpful to know that pamphlets are usually available which can provide you with more detailed information about your subject of interest. These pamphlets are often free or available for a small price from many agencies and organizations. Be sure to ask if the organization or agency has publications they can mail you. Because many of the organizations or agencies listed in this directory are national in scope, they will often direct you to their local affiliate for the specific assistance you may need.

YOUR LOCAL DIRECTORY

Your local telephone directory will list many people, government and private agencies (including federal, state, county and city), organizations and services that can help you in many situations and should be consulted first before using this directory. I suggest this only to save you time and the irritation caused, in many cases, by either getting through to your party or being passed on from person to person, department to department and agency to agency. Truly, your fingers can "do the walking."

GENERAL LEGAL ASSISTANCE

LEGAL AID SOCIETIES/NEIGHBORHOOD LEGAL ASSISTANCE/LEGAL SERVICES: Legal aid societies are funded by the federal government and usually are open only to lower income people. Legal aid lawyers handle a wide range of problems, including ones especially relevant to women such as sex discrimination in housing, credit and employment.

AMERICAN CIVIL LIBERTIES UNION: The ACLU is a national, nonprofit organization handling many types of civil right's problems, including women's rights. The ACLU has its own lawyers and maintains a referral service to other organizations and women's groups that handle specific problems.

CREATE YOUR OWN PERSONAL DIRECTORY

For your convenience, below you will find spaces where you can put important numbers and names you have contacted for future reference.

NAME: _____

PHONE: _____

CONTACT: _____

NAME: _____

PHONE: _____

CONTACT: _____

NAME: _____

PHONE: _____

CONTACT: _____

NAME: _____

PHONE: _____

CONTACT: _____

NAME: _____

PHONE: _____

CONTACT: _____

NAME: _____
PHONE: _____
CONTACT: _____

NAME: _____
PHONE: _____
CONTACT: _____

NAME: _____
PHONE: _____
CONTACT: _____

NAME: _____
PHONE: _____
CONTACT: _____

NAME: _____
PHONE: _____
CONTACT: _____

NAME: _____
PHONE: _____
CONTACT: _____

DIRECTORY OF 800 NUMBERS

The following is a list of 800 numbers for services, agencies and organizations which may be of service to you:

Abortion Referral Hotline-National Abortion Fed	800 772-9100
Acme Assoc. of Couples For Marriage-Enrichment	800 634-8325
Adoption Alliance	800 626-4324
Adoption By Gentle Care	800 824-9633
Adoption Center of California	800 637-7999
Adoption Center of Santa Barbara	800 432-2367
Adoption Law Center of Beverly Hills	800 932-2500
Adoption Services Associates	800 648-1807
Adoption World	800 233-1818
Adoption World	800 331-9393
Adoptions With Love	800 722-7731
Adult Education Hotline	800 642-2670
American Assoc. for Protecting Children	800 227-5242
American Woman's Economic Development	800 222-2933
American Woman's Medical Center	800 722-2636
Association of Trial Lawyers of America	800 424-2725
Association of Trial Lawyers of America-(Exchange)	800 344-3023
Bi-Weekly Mortgage Payment Service Co.	800 338-0764
Blind Children's Center Los Angles	800 222-3566
Business Law Help Line	800 874-3001
Child Abuse Prevention-Kids Peace	800 257-3223
Child Care Information	800 762-7929
Child Care Nutrition	800 634-3359
Child Care Placement Service (Nanny's)	800 338-1836
Child Care Resource & Referral	800 543-7382
Child Guard Information	800 323-9110
Child Care Partnership-Resource & Referral Center	800 782-1880

Child Help of Forester National-
Child Abuse Hotline .... 800 422-445?
Childquest (Nonprofit Recovery Children) .... 800 248-802(
Children's Rehabilitation Services .... 800 232-101?
College Aide (Student Loans) .... 800 322-825?
College Funds Database USA .... 800 348-647?
Development/Student Lifeline .... 800 842-990?
Compuserve .... 800 848-819?
Concern Employee Assistance Program .... 800 642-979?
Credit Card Protection Agency .... 800 826-166?
Credit Card Protection Agency .... 800 826-546?
Crime Stoppers .... 800 255-130?
Department of Labor & Industries .... 800 647-098?
Division On Aging (Information & Referral) .... 800 442-276?
Divorce Aid & Legal Resource Service .... 800 453-663?
Eastern Women's Center .... 800 346-511?
Estate-Guard Living Trust-
(Revocable Living Trust) .... 800 762-917?
Family Support & Information Network .... 800 852-004?
Farmers Assistance Counseling & Training-
Service (FACTS) .... 800 321-327?
Federal Tax Forms .... 800 829-367?
Friends of Children .... 800 643-212?
General Federation of Women's Clubs .... 800 443-439?
Healthy Mother Healthy Baby Line .... 800 422-296?
Help Call .... 800 435-722?
Helping Hands-
(Division of Childcare Connection) .... 800 544-626?
Hotline for the Handicapped .... 800 742-759?
Huntington Center for Independent Living .... 800 243-424?
Information .... 800 528-046?
Information Please .... 800 845-621?
Information Referrals & Crisis Help Line .... 800 233-435?
Institute for Black Parenting .... 800 367-885?
Institute for Stress Management .... 800 223-365?
Kennedy & Associates/Social Security-

Disability Advocacy 800 637-0593
Kevin Collins Foundation for Missing Children 800 272-0012
Kids Against Crime 800 522-5670
Kids USA (Child Abuse) 800 543-7025
Lawyer Referral-Nationwide Referral-
for Serious Injuries.. 800 622-9222
Louisiana child Care Association 800 241-1774
Mastercard-TDD Service for the Deaf 800 225-1208

Missing Children Safety Council National-
Child Watch Campaign.. 800 222-1464
MADD 800 248-6233
Mothers Centers... 800 645-3828
Mothers Helper Agency-Washington DC 800 942-2278
My Sisters Place... 800 443-3402
National AIDS Hotline Centers for-
Disease Control 800 342-2437
National AIDS Hotline-
(Hearing Impaired TTY)... 800 243-7889
National AIDS Hotline-
(Spanish) Centers for Disease Control 800 344-7432
National Assoc. for the Education-
of Young Children 800 424-2460
National Association for the Self Employed 800 232-6273
National Assn. of Latino Elected-
& Appointed Officials 800 446-2536
National Center for Missing-
& Exploited Children 800 843-5678
National Children's Cancer Society-
(Crisis Hotline).. 800 532-6459
National Credit Consumer Counseling 800 332-8123
National Farmers Organization 800 241-8808
National Farmers Organization 800 428-3276
National Fraud Information Center 800 876-7060
National Flood Insurance Program 800 638-6620
(For Hearing & Speech Impaired) 800 447-9487

North Side Women's Clinic 800 282-804
Northeast Career Schools 800 447-115
Ohio Protection & Advocacy Association 800 672-122
Ohio Victims of Crime Compensation Programs 800 824-826
Operation Lookout National Center-
for Missing Youth 800 782-733
Parent Care & Senior Support Service 800 352-735
Parent Identification Laboratory 800 433-684
Parental Stress Telephone Counseling Service 800 632-818
PC Help 800 368-071
PC Novice 800 848-147
Pennsylvania Coalition Against Rape 800 692-744
Pennsylvania Higher Education Assistance-
Agency Loans 800 692-739
Pennsylvania Higher Education Assistance-
Agency Grants 800 692-743
Pennsylvania Legal Services Center Inc. 800 322-757
People With AIDS Coalition Hotline 800 828-328
Personal Lawyer Network 800 356-627
Practical Parenting 800 255-337
Parkview Attorney Referral Services 800 252-996
Professional Resource Exchange 800 443-336
Project Locate 800 362-027
Public Interest Publications 800 537-935
Reproductive Services 800 227-398
Private Placement Adoption 800 345-918
Sanctuary Crisis Line 800 548-522
Scholarship Planning Institute 800 442-704
Scholarship Research Consultants 800 472-465
Scholarship Strategies 800 835-712
Scholarships for College 800 344-614
Scholastic Software Technical Assistance 800 548-160
Scientific Software 800 525-581
Self Insured Risk Services 800 482-272
Social Security Administration 800 772-121
Special Counsel for Immigration Related Unfair-

Employment Practices 800 255-7688
Surrogate Mothers Inc. 800 228-9066
Tax Planning Seminars 800 445-6914
Tax & Financial Strategies 800 253-0242
Tax School 800 327-1040
Tele Lawyer 800 835-3529
The Veterans Administration-
Medical Center DC 800 322-0254
The Woman Within 800 248-2000
Toys for Special Children 800 832-8697
U.S. Consumer Products Safety Commission-
Hotline 800 638-2772
U.S. Office of Special Counsel-
(Whistle Blowers) 800 572-2249
United States Department of Education 800 972-3186
U.S. Dept. of Commerce Fraud Waste & Abuse-
Hotline 800 424-5197
U.S. Federal Student Aid Infor Ctr, Dept of Ed 800 433-3243
U.S. Govt. Health Education & Welfare-
Student Finance 800 621-3115
U.S. Health & Human Services Dept.-Inspector 800 368-5779
U.S. Inspector Generals Hotline for Complaints-
of Fraud Waste or Abuse 800 424-4000
U.S. Office of Special Counsel DC 800 854-2824
U.S. Small Business Administration 800 624-7372
Vanished Children's Alliance 800 826-4743
Vietnam Veteran Family Assistance Programs 800 231-2606
Violent Crimes Compensation Board 800 242-0804
Volunteers of America Maternity
& Adoption Serv 800 535-9646
Washington Social & Health Services-
Office of Support Enforcement 800 345-9642
Women & Military Service for-
Memorial Foundation Inc. 800 222-2294
Women's Cancer Center 800 833-6253
Women's Health Care Services 800 882-0488

Women's Health Services 800 426-463

Every state has an office responsible for developing program
and policies benefiting older women. These offices provide fundin
for a wide variety of programs for older women, such as nutritio
programs, senior centers and legal services programs. Many stat
offices may operate some of these programs, in most instances the
forward funds to local governments and private organizations to er
able them to run these programs. If you have questions about wha
programs are available in your area, you can call your state office.

Alabama 205 261-574
Alaska 907 465-325
Arizona 602 255-444
Arkansas 501 371-244
California 916 322-529
Colorado 303 866-258
Connecticut 203 566-772
Delaware 302 421-679
District of Columbia 202 724-562
Florida 904 488-892
Georgia 404 894-533
Hawaii 808 548-259
Idaho 208 334-383
Illinois 217 785-335
Indiana 317 232-700
Iowa 515 281-518
Kansas 913 296-498
Kentucky 502 564-693
Louisiana 504 925-170
Maine 207 289-256
Maryland 301 383-506
Massachusetts 617 727-775
Michigan 517 373-823
Minnesota 612 296-254
Mississippi 601 354-659

Missouri	314 751-3082
Montana	406 444-3865
Nebraska	402 471-2306
Nevada	702 885-4210
New Hampshire	603 271-2751
New Jersey	609 292-4833
New Mexico	505 827-7640
New York	518 474-5731
North Carolina	919 733-3983
North Dakota	701 224-2577
Ohio	614 466-5500
Oklahoma	405 521-2281
Oregon	503 378-4728
Pennsylvania	717 783-1550
Rhode Island	401 277-2858
South Carolina	803 758-2576
South Dakota	605 773-3656
Tennessee	615 741-2056
Texas	512 475-2717
Utah	801 533-6422
Vermont	802 241-2400
Virginia	804 225-2271
Washington	206 753-2502
West Virginia	304 348-3317
Wisconsin	608 272-8606
Wyoming	307 777-7986

The following is a list of national legal programs specializing in the legal problems of the elderly. These organizations assist attorneys throughout the country on legal problems affecting older persons.

American Bar Assoc. Comm. on Legal-Problems of the Elderly	202 331-2297
Center for Social Gerontology	313 665-1126
Legal Counsel for the Elderly	202 662-4933

Do you have friends who would benefit from *Womens and Childrens Legal Rights Handbook?*

Call Monday thru Friday for Credit Card Orders
(9:00 am to 7:00 pm)
Or mail a copy of this order form.

Please send _____ copies of *Womens and Childrens Legal Rights Handbook* @ $14.95 ea.

$_____

North Carolina Residents add 6% sales tax
(90 cents per book)

$_____

Please add $2.00 for first book, $.50 for each additional book for shipping and handling.

$_____

Total $_____

_____

Name

_____

Address

_____

City, State, Zip

Send check or money order to:

Research Triangle Publishing
PO Box 1223
Fuquay-Variana, NC 27526
Toll Free at 800-941-0020